T0302716

on track ...
Laura
Nyro

every album, every song

Philip Ward

SONIC**BOND**

sonicbondpublishing.com

Sonicbond Publishing Limited
www.sonicbondpublishing.co.uk
Email: info@sonicbondpublishing.co.uk

First Published in the United Kingdom 2022
First Published in the United States 2022

British Library Cataloguing in Publication Data:
A Catalogue record for this book is available from the British Library

ISBN 978-1-78952-182-5

Typeset in ITC Garamond & ITC Avant Garde
Printed and bound in England

Graphic design and typesetting: Full Moon Media

on track ...
Laura Nyro

every album, every song

Philip Ward

sonicbondpublishing.com

Acknowlegements

As will be obvious, my biggest debt is to Laura's biographer, the late Michele Kort. Special thanks also to Jan Nigro, Madeline Sunshine, Jamie Christian, Andrew Batt, Sean McGhee, Mal Peachey, Lola Kirke, Peter Auker (for the pathway to Sondheim), Stephen Lambe (for commissioning the book) and to the online gang of fellow 'Nyrotics'.

Most of all, thank you, Laura, for the music.

on track ...

Laura Nyro

Contents

Introduction 9

More than a New Discovery (1967) 12

Eli and the Thirteenth Confession (1968) 24

New York Tendaberry (1969) 37

Christmas and the Beads of Sweat (1970) 48

Gonna Take a Miracle (1971) 59

Smile (1976) 71

Season of Lights... Laura Nyro in Concert (1977) 79

Nested (1978) 82

Mother's Spiritual (1984) 89

Laura: Laura Nyro Live at the Bottom Line (1989) 100

Walk the Dog & Light the Light (1993) 106

Angel in the Dark (2001) 115

The (Posthumous) Live Albums 125

Afterthoughts 130

Bibliography 132

Index of Song Titles 133

Introduction

Laura Nyro was one of the most significant American artists to emerge from the singer-songwriter boom of the 1960s. The roll-call of artists who have name-checked her with reverence is astounding for someone who is, alas, no longer a household name herself – Elton John, Elvis Costello, Linda Ronstadt, Todd Rundgren, Bob Dylan, Suzanne Vega, Neil Young, Renée Fleming. In 2012, Nyro was posthumously inducted into the Rock and Roll Hall of Fame. Despite this belated honour, she's never received as much attention as contemporaries like Joni Mitchell, Carole King and Carly Simon. Nyro's songs were recorded by Barbra Streisand, Blood, Sweat & Tears, Peter, Paul and Mary and many others, but it was on her own albums that she imprinted her vibrant, mercurial personality. This book is an attempt to tell her story through her recordings.

A native New Yorker, Laura Nyro was born in the Bronx on 18 October 1947. Her father Lou was a piano tuner and jazz trumpeter of mixed Russian Jewish and Italian Catholic heritage; her mother Gilda's people were originally Jewish immigrants from Ukraine. Late in life, Laura joked that the only proper reaction to life as an Italian Catholic Jew would be 'Oy vay Marone!': Yiddish and Neapolitan dialects combine in the linguistic melting pot of postwar New York. Her father loved the movie *Laura* – a great film noir of the 1940s, with its haunting theme tune by David Raksin – so 'Laura' she was named. At school, she seems to have been a reluctant pupil. She quit piano lessons at the age of eight because the teacher made her cry, and Laura had little formal training in music until she attended the High School of Music and Art in Manhattan as a teenager. Her lifelong friend Madeline Sunshine paints a picture of her at summer camp, aged 11 or 12: '...both wishing we weren't there and happy to sing the folk song 'Sloop John B' and raise our voices – mine froggy and hers extraordinary – on the chorus that said 'I want to go home...'.

With other friends, she formed harmony groups. Together they'd sing doo-wop in subway stations and on street corners, before Laura retreated to her bedroom to listen to records. Through her parents, she was exposed to a wide range of music. Her mother favoured opera singers and classical composers like Debussy and Ravel. Her father was a jazzman to his fingertips, guiding her towards John Coltrane and Miles Davis. Girl groups, Motown, Brill Building pop, Broadway musicals: her musical inheritance was as varied as her ethnic background. From an early age, she was reading poetry and writing songs. She was also a talented painter, mainly in watercolours. In later life, she looked back on this as a joyful time, though there must have been dark moments too. In a 1969 TV interview (from which only the audio survives), she reflected on her moody adolescent self, noting that what doesn't kill us can make us stronger. Art has that saving power: 'Sometimes I'd just be in my room, totally tuned out, or totally tuned in to my own thing, because in my world I could look at my pain and it wasn't ugly to me. It was a matter of understanding it and channelling it into a beautiful thing'. In the same interview, she admitted, 'I think I see things differently than most people'. This was apparent from early on and would become a hallmark of her art.

The family name was 'Nigro' (pronounced 'nigh-gro'). Ever the individualist, Laura tried out various alternatives, finally settling on 'Nyro' (It rhymes with 'hero'); the 'NY' syllable perhaps in recognition of her native city. She developed a quirky fashion sense to go with her distinctive name – hemlines trailing the ground when other girls were hitching them above the knee, big tinny clusters of fake pearls. It was, one early profile suggested, the look of a 'Spanish fortune teller': long black hair, dark, deep-set eyes, full lips atop a *zaftig* figure. And with it all went an obsessive taste for tuna fish sandwiches.

From the start, the music was as personalised as the look. In the mid-1960s, there was little precedent for women writing and performing their own music. A professional songwriter like Carole King would 'demo' a song in the expectation that someone else would then record and release it. Laura started out in a similar vein. She told *Downbeat* magazine at the time: 'I wasn't interested in singing my music, but I thought maybe I wanted other people to do it'. Indeed, her early successes came when established recording artists began covering her songs. But no one sang them with the authority of their author, and producers soon realised this. Her opulent vocals and idiosyncratic changes of tempo and dynamics were integral to the song meanings; likewise her untutored sense of harmony. Charlie Calello, who produced her album *Eli and the Thirteenth Confession*, has described how she approached piano chords quite unlike most rock musicians he'd worked with: 'She would play triads, but she would play the *wrong* bass notes, which would make the chords. She would play major-9th chords without the 3rds'. Since, in root position, the 3rd is what defines a chord as major or minor, this habit created ambiguity and tension. Later on, when her style ossified, this became something of a mannerism, but at the outset of her career it was refreshingly new. She suffered (or profited) from a condition called synaesthesia, which must have something to do with it: she heard music as colours, as a chromatic palette to dip into, not as dots on a page.

My own journey towards Laura began as a teenager in Britain. A couple of her tracks appeared on sampler albums issued by CBS for the UK market. In her music I found a frantic synthesis of so many of the musical styles I was coming to appreciate. I never expected to find them together in one place, and the mystery was compounded when I found them in someone about as far removed from my nerdy suburban self as it was possible to get. But it is to her that I owe my lifelong passion for women singer-songwriters. The voice – alternately soothing and shrill, ranging unfettered over several octaves – was not quite of this world. Later in life, her music loosened up (to its detriment, in my view) and she'd refer to this early work as 'a little crazy'. But to a young man ill-at-ease in his own skin, it was a revelation. 'Sometimes

I feel like a mirror in a storm: a mirror that's smashed against the earth', she told interviewer Chris Albertson in 1970. The quote captures the fractured interiority of those first albums. After a brief retirement in the 1970s, she returned, audibly in transition from the exhilarating wildness of her late-1960s heyday to the socially conscious earth mother of later years. While I retain my preference for the early albums, my older self also finds something of value in this calmer, later work. Happily, her vocal bravura and inimitable way with keyboard harmony remained intact until her untimely death in 1997. And the ethos of the *On Track* series is to treat every album with respect – so, reader, I'll do my best.

This book aims to discuss every Laura Nyro song that's seen the light of day. There will inevitably be more about the earlier albums than the later, not only because her best-known songs date from that era, but because it's on the early albums that she's at her most innovative: defying expectation, courting the unconventional. What I realise now – but barely intuited on first hearing – is that these albums (*Eli and the Thirteenth Confession* and *New York Tendaberry*, in particular) lie at a cusp of 1960s music. It was a time when women were transitioning from being either a singer with the band or a soloist performing songs written by professional songwriters to – in Laura's case – the empowered singer-songwriter figure who emerged at the end of the decade. She was in the vanguard of that movement whose consequences resonate down to the present. Hers is a quintessentially American music. It sweeps up some of the most distinctive styles invented or perfected in America and filters them through a unique sensibility. Many of these were hybrid styles to begin with, so her accomplishment was to forge a personal idiom out of extreme hybridity. If I focus equally on the lyrics, it's because she was a poet as well as a musician. She told journalist Paul Zollo in 1994: 'Sometimes the meaning of a lyric is in the sound of a lyric, and sometimes there's a more straightforward lyric'. I try to bear that advice in mind.

With other artists who've passed to the studio in the sky, we must face a *post mortem* flood of alternative takes and unreleased material. This seems not to be the case with Laura: in later life she got into the habit of erasing or destroying her outtakes. What survives is what she wanted us to hear. And what a legacy it is.

More than a New Discovery (1967)

Personnel:
Laura Nyro: vocals
The Hi Fashions (Dolores Woods, Fatimah Halim), Linda November, Leslie Miller,
Toni Wine: background vocals
Jay Berliner, Al Gorgoni, Bucky Pizzarelli: guitar
Stan Free: piano
Bill LaVorgna: drums
Toots Thielemans, Buddy Lucas: harmonica
Lou Mauro: double bass
Jimmy Sedlar: trumpet
Herb Bernstein: arranger, conductor, flugelhorn
Recorded at Bell Sound Studios, New York City, July/November 1966
Producer: Milt Okun
Production Supervisor: Jerry Schoenbaum
Production Assistant: Jean Goldhirsch
Director of engineering: Val Valentin
Engineer: Harry Yarmark
Label: Verve Folkways
Release date: February 1967 (US)
Chart place: US: did not chart (1973 reissue peaked at 97 in US)
Running time: 36:15
Current edition: Rev-Ola 2008 CD

Self-belief swept the teenage Laura from aspirant to recording artist. In the
early-1960s, Artie Mogull – an A&R man at Warner Bros. – signed Bob Dylan
to his first music publishing contract. When the contract ended, Mogull quit
Warner and went into the music publishing business on his own, taking
Dylan with him. He tells the story of how, one day in 1966, Laura's father
came to tune the piano in the publisher's office and took the opportunity to
sing his daughter's praises. Lou Nigro's persistence paid off. Mogull agreed to
audition her: 'Next day, this little, short, unattractive girl comes up, and the
first three songs she plays are 'Wedding Bell Blues', 'Stoney End', and then
'And When I Die'. I almost fainted. I went crazy.' Whatever his reservations
about her appearance, Mogull was sufficiently impressed to put her under
contract, and arranged a meeting with producer Milt Okun to record a
demo tape. The tape – containing several songs she never committed to
disc – survives and was officially released on CD and vinyl in 2021 as *Go
Find the Moon: The Audition Tape*. It provides early evidence of how the
musical decision-makers just didn't *get* her. We hear Mogull try to pressure
her into performing 'standards' as an alternative to her own unorthodox
compositions. She resists. Okun was struck by her talent, but felt her songs
needed structure. He made it a condition of their working together that
they smooth out the irregularities of shape and tempo, to arrive at a more

commercial product. She met the same reaction from Herb Bernstein, who was brought in as arranger for the planned album. Meanwhile, Mogull had found a niche for Laura with Verve Folkways, an MGM-owned label that was looking to supplement its folk roster with more pop-oriented acts. Recording took place over two sessions in July and November 1966.

Laura doesn't play piano on the album. Later in her career, it would be vital to her self-expression that she accompany herself, but this was one of many compromises forced upon her if her music was ever to reach the public's ears. Okun, believing her sense of rhythm was too erratic for Bernstein's arrangements, brought in pianist Stan Free. The other players were all seasoned New York session men. Backing vocals were led by a three-woman group Bernstein had worked with before, The Hi Fashions. At the time, studios were limited to 4 or 8-track recording. In this case it was 4-track, and this limitation and the restricted budget forced Bernstein to be inventive, often using no more than four or five instruments per song, with little scope for overdubbing to thicken the sound. Bernstein took a decidedly-commercial line on some numbers – including 'Stoney End' and 'Wedding Bell Blues' – but allowed Laura's unique artistry more freedom on other songs: notably ballads such as 'Lazy Susan', 'I Never Meant To Hurt You' and 'He's A Runner'.

Though at the time Laura played the game and did as she was told, she was evidently unhappy with the results. Looking back, she told *Downbeat* magazine in April 1970 how Bernstein had knocked out about six arrangements in three hours, eviscerating all subtlety from her hard-won effort: 'I mean, I work months and hours and years and a lifetime on my songs, and if something was a bit difficult, he'd just chop it right out… like if one of my changes was a bit difficult. They really kind of brought down my music.'

In fact, the album stands up well enough. It showcases the range of Laura's influences and her songwriting talent, and she delivers some visceral and truly soulful vocals. In a sense, the money men were vindicated. Laura's songs – regularised, flattened out by commercial interests – were soon being picked up elsewhere, and this album would supply more hits for other artists than any of her later albums. The publishing royalties were assured, even if she'd been denied the chance to record *her* songs as she conceived them. Within little more than a year, it would be a different story.

In an effort to broaden the label's appeal, in 1967, Verve Folkways rebranded itself as Verve Forecast. Laura's first album was reissued under that imprint in 1969, at which point it was retitled, the cover design changed, and the tracks reordered to put the (by then) most familiar tracks first and last:

Side One: 'Wedding Bell Blues', 'Billy's Blues', 'California Shoeshine Boys', 'Blowin' Away', 'Lazy Susan', 'Goodbye Joe'
Side Two: 'Hands Off The Man (Flim Flam Man)', 'Stoney End', 'I Never Meant To Hurt You', 'He's A Runner', 'Buy And Sell', 'And When I Die'

After Laura's move to her long-term label Columbia, they reissued the album – now titled *The First Songs* – with yet another change of cover, but with the original track order restored. One wonders whose decision it was to reorder the tracks. By 1969, Laura was taking control of her work in a way she'd been denied hitherto. However, her later indifference to the album, her tendency in interviews to refer to *Eli and the Thirteenth Confession* as her 'first' album, and the restoration of the original running order in 1973, all suggest that these decisions were out of her hands.

'Goodbye Joe' (Laura Nyro)

Released as a single A-side, 25 February 1967, b/w 'Billy's Blues'
Released as a single A-side, October 1969, b/w 'I Never Meant To Hurt You'
In some ways, a song of valediction is a strange way to open an album, but it's typical of Laura's lyrics that we cannot be sure how she feels about Joe's departure from her life. 'Joe' is the first of several named figures on the album. It would be naïve to identify him, or the others, with any one individual. However, the lyric suggests an affair that began out of town – 'on the highland', among the deer – and continues, perhaps ends, in the city (Manhattan). Whether or not the relationship ended by mutual consent, either way, Joe's 'got to go'. Laura is 'trying not to cry', but stoically she recognises that 'time is full of changes'. Perhaps this is a new beginning, hence the track's pole position. (On the 1969 reissue, the tracks were reordered. 'Goodbye Joe' became the last track on side one, perhaps a more appropriate point to say goodbye, or at least *au revoir*. But as we've suggested, it's unlikely that Laura had much say over sequencing.)

   The first of the album's 'rollicking shuffle-beat numbers' (in Nyro biographer Michele Kort's phrase) features the vocal trio prominently on the title line, and some overemphatic brass. Following 'Wedding Bell Blues', it was the album's second single, released at a time when Verve were still struggling to position Laura as a pop artist. 'That 'Wedding Bell Blues' gal has lost another man and found another hit!' ran the cringeworthy advertising copy for the single. Despite their efforts, and unlike the album's other tracks, this one wasn't picked up by other artists, apart from an amiable version by jazz artist Carmen McRae, with The Dixie Flyers, on McRae's 1970 album *Just a Little Lovin'*.

'Billy's Blues' (Laura Nyro)

Released as a single B-side, 25 February 1967, b/w 'Goodbye Joe'
After the upbeat opening track, the mood turns melancholy. Chimes introduce this beautiful ballad, presented in a spare arrangement built around piano and guitar. To this, Bernstein added what he called a 'bluesy trumpet thing right out of a nightclub', establishing a smoky atmosphere, like the trails of a dozen cigarettes. Speaking about the album later, Bernstein mentioned an unintended edit that crept in after his work was done. He'd ended his arrangement as it had begun, with two chimes. They disappeared in the final

cut. The listener doesn't know that, and in fact, the song ending on Laura's unaccompanied voice is hugely effective.

It's an astonishingly mature vocal for a 19-year-old. Little wonder that those who first heard the teenage Laura thought she must be a much older woman. The sustained vowel sounds, the careful placing of final consonants, the breath control: these are all the hallmarks of an experienced singer.

Structurally more conventional than many of her later songs and relying on full rhymes (shoes/blues/lose), 'Billy's Blues' even boasts a contrasting B section ('Some folks have it good'). But the lyric tells a consistent tale throughout – Billy is down and in need of consolation; a song will do it, or someone to 'right the wrong'. One suspects the influence of Harold Arlen – an overlooked Broadway master best-remembered for 'Over The Rainbow', but whose most characteristic work was a kind of stately reimagining of the blues in songs like 'Blues In The Night' and 'The Man That Got Away'.

'And When I Die' (Laura Nyro)
Released as a single B-side, 29 April 1967, b/w 'Flim Flam Man'
Released as a single A-side, March 1969, b/w 'I Never Meant to Hurt You'
If 'Billy's Blues' showcased the precocity of Laura's vocal powers, the next track gives us Laura the songwriting prodigy. Written when she was only 16, this gem is among her earliest compositions. After a slow intro, the song settles into a breezy gospel number, using the full brass section and a tack piano. Recurrent *blue* notes disturb the basic C-major tonality. It's as if she's back in the world of teenage summer camps. It was one of the songs she auditioned for Artie Mogull in 1966, in a performance strikingly close to this studio recording made the following year, even down to the chuckle as she sings about burial ('It's *cold* way down there').

Many teenagers are preoccupied with death; many are sustained by the belief they will live forever. It was Laura's insight that the contradictory claims of pessimism and optimism could be loaded into one song. The lyric covers a surprising amount of ground in somewhat under three minutes. Laura sings: as long as she's living, she demands freedom ('no chains on me'). When it's over, she hopes for a natural death. She's uncertain about an afterlife – swears there's no heaven, prays there's no hell – but recognises that only death will settle the matter. What's certain is that she doesn't want to 'die uneasy', or go by the Devil, the demon or Satan – an anticipation in this early lyric of diabolic figures who will loom large in her New York trilogy. However, in the buoyant chorus, optimism for the future, breaks through: confidence that when she's gone, 'There'll be one child born/And a world to carry on'.

Milt Okun – always with an eye to the market – arranged the song for folk trio Peter, Paul and Mary: a version that appeared in August 1966, some months before Laura's own recording. But it was the later cover by Blood, Sweat & Tears – released as a single in late-1969 – that took the song stratospheric. Their jazz-inflected recording reached number 2 on the US *Billboard* Hot

100, deprived of the top spot only by The Beatles' double A-side 'Come Together'/'Something'. Laura was generous about these covers. She said hearing other people sing her songs was 'just like an ice-cream soda; a lively high, a very sweet feeling'. This one was still packing a punch in 2000 when it turned up in a funeral scene of the hit TV series *Ally McBeal*. As ditzy lawyer Ally buries her long-term sweetheart – the aptly named 'Billy' – she speaks lines from the song before the church choir break into a full-throated gospel rendition.

In later years Laura slightly distanced herself from the song. As she told interviewer Scott Simon in 1989, it seemed to express the 'folk wisdom that teenagers have'; they're in touch with a 'very primal truth'. But she continued to sing it until the end of her life. In a live recording from the Bottom Line, New York, in summer 1988, she reharmonises it with the characteristic open chords of her mature style while omitting the verse with Satanic references. Her worldview had changed a lot in 30 years.

When Laura was posthumously inducted into the Rock and Roll Hall of Fame in 2012, her son Gil Bianchini accepted the award on her behalf. Bette Midler, after a teary tribute worthy of an Oscar acceptance speech, introduced him as 'the one child born'. Midler could be assured that many in the audience would recognise the quotation.

'Stoney End' (Laura Nyro)

Released as a single B-side, 17 September 1966, b/w 'Wedding Bell Blues'
Released as a single A-side, November 1968, b/w 'Flim Flam Man'

Despite the various Jewish and Catholic elements in her background, Laura's upbringing was not especially religious. When she was about eight, her parents sent her to Sunday classes at New York's Ethical Culture School. The Ethical Culture movement, founded by Felix Adler in the late-19th century, offered a secular alternative to organised religion. Adler believed that morality should be independent of theology, and the movement attempted to provide a universal fellowship devoid of ritual and ceremony for those who would otherwise be divided by creeds. Laura would later pay credit to the education she received there.

The early grounding in humanist values is relevant to Laura's use of religious imagery. 'Stoney End' is the first of her great *character* songs. She projects herself into an 'I' figure who is her and yet is not her. The character in the song has had a solid Christian upbringing ('raised on the good book Jesus') but has lost her faith. Disillusioned in romance, she seeks sanctuary in her mother's arms ('Mama cradle me again'). The lyric makes poetic use of parallelism – the 'broken thunder' in the sky matches the state of her soul; the sunrise reflects the 'lovelight' in the lover's eyes. And central to the whole is the image of '*the* stoney end' – not, as some listeners assume, a place name with initial capital letters, but a metaphorical location; a place she 'never wanted to go'; somewhere the relationship took her to. Some hear an allusion to religious cultures where a woman could be stoned for sexual transgression (the fate threatening the 'woman taken in adultery' in the New Testament until Jesus intervenes with his gospel of compassion), but this is surely too determinate a reading. The line is deliberately ambiguous.

One of her most accessible melodies, 'Stoney End' was recorded at the first sessions in July 1966, together with 'Wedding Bell Blues'. A different take must've been recorded on the same day, as the single version has some notable lyric changes. Gone is mention of the 'good book Jesus', replaced by 'golden rules'. The poor mother no longer works the 'mines', and the singer now suffers heartache at the hands of a 'winsome Johnny'. These changes (for the worse) were undoubtedly imposed on Laura in the effort to secure airplay and avoid offending the God-fearing: a vain effort since the single failed to break into the *Billboard* Hot 100. Like so many of Laura's songs, it owes its commercial success to another performer. Barbra Streisand made it the title track of her 1971 album. Her single version reached number six on the *Billboard* early that year and became the diva's second top-10 hit. This was more of a rock arrangement than Laura's; inevitably bigger, the tempo slightly faster. But Laura's original carries more conviction. Streisand continues to include the song in her repertoire, even if she doesn't claim to understand it. 'What's a stoney end?' she asks the audience rhetorically in one concert recording from 2006. She guessed it must be 'kind of metaphorical and abstract'.

'Lazy Susan' (Laura Nyro)
The musician Alan Merrill was a neighbour of Laura's when she was growing up and was a relation on her mother's side. He offered insights into several of the early songs. He believes 'Lazy Susan' was inspired by his feelings for one Susan Shapiro. As he explained to Laura's biographer Michele Kort: 'I was always talking about Susan to Laura, obsessively. Laura craved a close, loving relationship with that sort of intensity for herself. She felt that Susan just had things come to her so easily, and envied her'.

The track seems to describe a character of that sort. Susan has got her man without undue effort. The singer has lost hers. The last verse suggests they may be one and the same man – 'Johnny' – who is discovered 'up there on the hillside' with lazy Susan. But whatever experience may have prompted the lyric, Laura translates the situation from the *personal* to the *natural* world. The name Susan contains a whole bouquet of floral connections, deriving ultimately from Persian and Hebrew words for 'lily'. More precisely – and Laura puns explicitly on this – 'lazy Susan' is one of the colloquial names for 'black-eyed Susan' (*Rudbeckia hirta*), a flowering plant native to eastern and central North America. It has yellow petals circling a brown or black cone, giving the impression of a black eye. It likes the sun and attracts the butterflies, much as the girl in the song – 'black-eyed Sue' – has nothing to do but 'sit there/And light up the hillside'. (*Rudbeckia* is also the state flower of Maryland – perhaps some private code is intended, closing the circle of reference from the natural back to the personal world.)

Laura is in appropriately laid-back mood for this gentle, slow ballad, teasing out the long vowels. The opening on dramatic chords and low strings illustrates how Bernstein's arrangements strive for 'big' effects with the limited personnel at his disposal. This is one of the album's more successful orchestrations and marks the first appearance of Toots Thielemans on chromatic harmonica. It was quite a coup to get the Belgian-born jazzman – who'd worked with everyone from Benny Goodman to Miles Davis – to grace a debut album by an unknown artist. Bernstein has described how he wrote a little for Thielemans, and then simply let him improvise. Successful as the track is, the listener may still be drawn back to Laura's original demo with piano alone (on *Go Find the Moon*): it's slower still, and darker, and brooding.

'Hands Off The Man' (Laura Nyro)

Released as a single A-side (under the title 'Flim Flam Man'), 29 April 1967, b/w 'And When I Die'
Released as a single B-side (under the title 'Flim Flam Man'), November 1968, b/w 'Stoney End'
Released as a single B-side (under the title 'Flim Flam Man'), February 1973, b/w 'Wedding Bell Blues'

After the heady floral essence of 'Lazy Susan', we're back to the upbeat knockabout charm of the album's opening track. Alan Merrill believes this song – later retitled 'Flim Flam Man' – was inspired by Laura's Uncle Gary: a charmer and ladies' man, a guy whose ambition ran ahead of his abilities. An alternative suggestion is that it was written for the 1967 movie *The Flim-Flam Man* (hence the later retitling): perhaps submitted speculatively to the producers, but not used. At the outset of Laura's career, when she was focused on marketing her songs to other people, this is the sort of thing she would've done. In the movie, George C. Scott played a rural con artist in the American South (a flim-flam man), who takes on a young army deserter as his *protégé* and teaches him the tricks of the trade. The folky score of the completed film was written by Jerry Goldsmith; there's no evidence that Laura's name was ever attached to the project.

The vocal is confident, self-assured, joyous: appropriate to celebrating a proverbial 'bad boy'. Whatever unwelcome pressures Laura was placed under during the recording process, it sounds as if she's enjoying herself here. The lyrics are equally playful: the half-rhyme of 'Trojan horse' and 'Santa Claus' is witty; 'His mind is up his sleeve' perfectly captures the devious misuse of inborn intelligence. The backing singers, led by the Hi Fashions, are powerfully deployed to drive home the title line.

Laura's single version, the third single carved from *More than a New Discovery*, failed to chart. Once again, it was left to Barbra Streisand to take the song where Laura had been unable to. Streisand's single from her *Stoney*

End album reached number 82 on the US *Billboard* Hot 100 in early-1971. (A 1968 cover by Peggy Lipton, future wife of Quincy Jones, is also worth seeking out.)

'Wedding Bell Blues' (Laura Nyro)
Released as a single A-side, 17 September 1966, b/w 'Stoney End'. US: 103
Released as a single A-side, February 1973, b/w 'Flim Flam Man'
Recorded at the album's first session alongside 'Stoney End', 'Wedding Bell Blues' makes for a rousing opener to side two of the original album (On the 1969 re-release it was promoted to the start of side one). Another precocious product of the teenage Laura's imagination, this was one of the songs that made her name. Its relative structural simplicity may have helped in that respect. In a 1984 interview with Bruce Pollock of *Guitar* magazine, she implied as much: 'I have a love for simple, basic song structure, although sometimes you'd never know it. Take for example, 'Wedding Bell Blues' – a three-minute song with a simple hook: the universe captured in a three-minute song, like a painting on a page'.

Harmonically, it's typical of much of her early music, in combining the familiar II-V-I pattern of generations of American songsmiths with a modal stepwise movement of 7th chords up and down the scale: the latter surely suggested by the movement of the pianist's hands on the keyboard. Buddy Lucas' bluesy harmonica amplifies the title's blues theme. The lyric is more direct than many of her later songs, although she allows herself a flight of poetic fancy with the alliterative phrase 'choir of carousels'.

Alan Merrill claims the song is about his mother Helen's affair with a married man, a B-movie actor named Bill. Helen herself, frustrated at being unable to marry him, confirmed the claim. But Laura turned it into everyone's story. Ever since then, when a girl had a boyfriend called Bill, if he was slow to step up to the mark, she could invoke this song and call radio stations, requesting it to be played. However, the version played was more likely to be the cover by The 5th Dimension, which reached number 1 in the US in November 1969. Their version was also a top-20 hit in Britain. For many sex-starved British males, their first exposure to Laura's music on television, albeit unwittingly, was when girl dance troupe Pan's People – a vision in white polyester – brought their painfully literal choreography to The 5th Dimension hit on *Top of the Pops* in January 1970. More recently, the song has found a new British champion in ex-Smiths frontman Morrissey, whose single version was released in 2019. According to his label's press release, Morrissey's take on the song entails 'injecting the classic ode to frustrated love with a modern, polished euphoria that subtly nods at queer desire'. Well, I never.

Laura's own single release, which peaked just outside the Hot 100, was promoted with a crass advert showing her reluctantly squeezed into a wedding dress, with the tag 'Not every girl gets her man to say I do'. Within a few months, she would take control of her music and her image.

'Buy And Sell' (Laura Nyro)

A complete change of mood now. This beautiful sultry ballad is one of the most undervalued of Laura's early compositions. Perhaps its somewhat louche subject matter denied it wider currency – unlike other tracks on the album, it wasn't picked up by other artists at the time (Suzanne Vega's notable cover dates from the late-1990s). The subject seems to be the prostitute's life: she who must sell her 'goods' to buy her 'roof'. What are these goods? 'My bed' is apparently where they are delivered, so the answer is not hard to find. Around this shadowy figure, Laura sketches in details of urban life – laughing children, finely dressed ladies, 'cocaine and quiet beers' – against a cosmic backdrop of life rolling forward and death pulling us back like a 'vesper bell'. In condensed form, the song offers an early glimpse of the cityscape that will unfold over the next three albums.

The arrangement is appropriately spare. Pianist Stan Free provides a simple chordal foundation, laying down a pattern reminiscent of Erik Satie's famous 'Gymnopédie', before easing into cocktail-jazz mode for the faster bridge. Jimmy Sedlar's muted horn fades in and out behind Laura's languid vocal before the track comes to rest on a single low F from the piano. Laura was someone who had Broadway song in her bloodstream. There could be an afterglow here of Cole Porter's great memorial to the oldest profession, 'Love For Sale'.

'He's A Runner' (Laura Nyro)

Some men are 'keepers', some are 'runners'. This soulful track is emphatically about the latter. It's another of her earliest compositions which she thought worthy to commit to disc. And she was right. It's a classic, which, surprisingly, wasn't picked up by other artists (with the exception of Mama Cass in 1970). Alan Merrill recalls recording an early demo of the song with Laura even before she'd entered Milt Okun's orbit. (Merrill played blues harp against her piano. The demo hasn't survived.)

The album arrangement again features Thieleman's jazz harmonica, with percussion more to the fore (Bill LaVorgna's eruptive bongos). Rather like 'Buy And Sell', Laura moves into a faster bridge in the middle, which culminates in a wailing cry of 'Now I'm in chains/Till I die'. Death and dying – even if only invoked for rhetorical effect – will be an abiding preoccupation for this young woman. The outer verses seem to warn the sisterhood off the philanderer; in the bridge, she gets personal: she's part of his trail of destruction.

'He's A Runner' was one of two songs Laura performed on the January 1969 NBC-TV special *Kraft Music Hall Presents the Sound of the Sixties*, hosted by Bobby Darin. In one of her few surviving TV appearances, she sits on the piano stool and delivers a cool, measured vocal live against a pre-recorded backing track. Always reluctant to appear on screen, she avoids the camera, seeming to insulate herself against self-consciousness by losing herself in the intensity of song.

'Blowin' Away' (Laura Nyro)

A moment of unbuttoned joy and relief between the weightier tracks that surround it, 'Blowin' Away' shows us Laura's other side, her playful side. Her brother Jan feels that critics and biographers sometimes lose sight of her sense of humour. He told me: 'Laura's public persona was quiet and mysterious, and somewhat serious, but I can remember so many times of the two of us laughing and joking. It was a lot of fun for me to make her laugh'.

Some hear the song as a celebration of sex; others assume the singer is feeling so 'high' because she's on illicit substances. Its unique feature is that Laura stands down the backing singers here in favour of multitracking her own vocals. This would become her common practice on later albums, but in this instance, where the studio was still limited to four-track recording, it involved careful mixing down before the instruments and lead vocal could be added on the remaining tracks.

Not for the first time, Laura channels the sound of early-1960s R&B vocal groups like The Orlons. With its down-home oom-pah rhythm and vaguely trippy lyrics, 'Blowin' Away' ranks for this listener alongside 'California Shoeshine Boys' as among the less convincing tracks on the record. Nonetheless, like several of her other songs, it was picked up at the time by The 5th Dimension, whose single version climbed to number 21 on the *Billboard* chart in February 1970.

'I Never Meant To Hurt You' (Laura Nyro)

Released as a single B-side, March 1969, b/w 'And When I Die'
Released as a single B-side, October 1969, b/w 'Goodbye Joe'
After the ebullience of 'Blowin' Away', the mood shifts for another reflective ballad that sounds like an instant jazz standard. It's the sort of number you could imagine Sarah Vaughan – one of Laura's early idols – singing, though perhaps in a less leaden arrangement than it receives here at Herb Bernstein's hands. In a notebook she kept after leaving school in 1965, Laura jotted down a series of what appear to be song titles. One of them was 'Never Meant To Hurt You'. We cannot be sure if this was the same composition she went on to record in late-1966 (with the addition of a personal pronoun to the title), but if so, we have here another of her earliest completed songs. That would excuse – if excuse were needed – its slightly derivative style.

As always, we should be wary of identifying the 'I' of the song with Laura's personal circumstances. She speaks for anyone who regrets a careless word spoken in anger or pique; the way little things in a relationship can fracture the bigger picture. Self-concealment will be a recurrent theme in Laura's lyrics: this character has 'a heart that hides its face'. Her next album will trace the alternation of concealment and self-revelation through an entire song cycle.

'California Shoeshine Boys' (Laura Nyro)

The album ends with an amiable shuffle-beat number, featuring some energetic harmonica work from Buddy Lucas. These boys are cut from the same cloth as the flim-flam man: they're bad news – notching up girls on their bedposts – but still fatally attractive; they can shine the singer's shoes anytime. After some of the highs experienced earlier on the album, it's a disappointing close. The reordering in 1969 relegated this negligible song to the middle of side one, preferring to close side two with 'And When I Die'. Generally, one would value the original release over any reissue, but in this case, the later decision made good sense.

Contemporary Tracks
'Enough Of You' (Laura Nyro)
Released on *Go Find the Moon* (CD, 2021)
The 1966 audition tape includes three original songs that Laura never recorded for album release (or four if we include 'Luckie'). They show how her style arrived almost fully formed. She still assumes she's showcasing songs that would be picked up by others, but her delivery is so distinctive and mature – the free-ranging vocal, the symbiosis of piano and voice, the slowing and speeding-up – that you can't imagine anyone else singing them. 'Enough Of You' is a languid, smoky ballad with a jazz edge. She slides into *blue* notes like a seasoned professional. Admittedly, the lyric is less personal than what would come later – as if she's generalising in the effort to fit a genre: it's constructed like one of those Broadway-show songs where the singer asks herself if she can leave her man ('Now haven't I had enough of you?') before concluding that she can't ('Never could I ever/Have enough of you'). At the end, you long to stand up and applaud. Instead, we hear Mogull's voice from the control booth, simply asking Laura if she wants to 'rest a while'.

'In And Out' (Laura Nyro)
Released on *Go Find the Moon* (CD, 2021)
Laura had no wish to 'rest a while'. She wanted to try this chirpy, upbeat little number. She doesn't get very far before giving up, but far enough to give the idea. Love has thrown her into confusion: she doesn't know if she's in or out of it. The words tumble out in punning playfulness: 'One day I'm in up to my chin/But all in doubt/I look about/And all within/I'm down and out'. If the lyrics are Cole Porter, the music is boogie-woogie. Many were the influences at work on the teenage Laura. If this track sounds less like the songwriter of later years, it's because those influences were not yet wholly assimilated.

An acetate surfaced a few years ago featuring a (possibly) complete performance of this song. Here it emerges with a more dramatic structure: there's a characteristic deceleration near the end leading to a finale of hammered chords. Whatever its provenance – the acetate label credits the 'Peer/Southern Organization' – it sounds like she's having fun.

'Go Find The Moon' (Laura Nyro)
Released on *Go Find the Moon* (CD, 2021)
It's curious that, in the 1966 audition, Mogull asked her whether she knew any pop standards, because it's evident from her self-penned songs that she did. Unprepared and unrehearsed, she may not have made much headway with 'When Sunny Gets Blue', 'Kansas City' or 'I Only Want To Be With You' – the three songs she attempted in response to his persistent requests – but she'd absorbed their lessons. As well as carefully rhymed lyrics, 'Go Find The Moon' has the fluent chord progression and walking bass pattern familiar from professional songsmiths of the 1950s. (Perhaps from earlier still; Michele Kort describes it as 'Geshwinesque'.) Laura's performance here is intuitive, unfettered. Sure, the words are a little bland compared to later work. She hasn't escaped the old 'moon/June' clichés. We have 'I'll pocket a star fresh from June' followed by 'So baby, better wear your hair down/And you go find the moon'. But 'Go Find the Moon' wouldn't sound amiss in any jazz club. In fact, under the title 'The Moon Song', it has found a place in the repertoire of contemporary New York singer-songwriter Marion LoGuidice.

'Luckie' (Laura Nyro)
Released on *Go Find the Moon* (CD, 2021)
Not the song of the same title that appears on *Eli and the Thirteenth Confession*, but something else altogether. It's possibly an early draft of the same ideas. Both songs refer to 'dead end zones' and lucky clover; both include the line 'Luckie's takin' over'. But instead of the menacing Devil and mysterious Captain who populate the later song, this one leans on more conventional personification: the antagonists had a showdown last night and 'Luckie sent Trouble on his way'. She's been down but now she's up; Fortune's wheel has turned. Later she'd wrap up this simple message in opaque imagery and hazy chords. Here it stands proud, an expression of independence of spirit from a young woman auditioning for an older man who'd rather hear 'Moon River'.

Eli and the Thirteenth Confession (1968)

Personnel:
Laura Nyro: vocals, piano, harmonies, 'witness to the confession'
Ralph Casale, Chet Amsterdam: acoustic guitar
Hugh McCracken: electric guitar
Chuck Rainey, Chet Amsterdam: bass
Artie Schroeck: drums, vibes
Buddy Saltzman: drums
Dave Carey: percussion
Bernie Glow, Pat Calello, Ernie Royal: trumpet
George Young, Zoot Sims: saxophone
Wayne Andre, Jimmy Cleveland, Ray DeSio: trombone
Joe Farrell: saxophone, flute
Paul Griffin: piano on 'Eli's Comin'' and 'Once It Was Alright Now (Farmer Joe)'
Recorded at Columbia Studios, New York City, January/February 1968
Producers: Charlie Calello, Laura Nyro
Arranger: Charlie Calelo
Engineers: Roy Segal, Stan Tonkel
Label: Columbia
Release date: 13 March 1968 (US), August 1968 (UK)
Chart place: US: 181
Running time: 46:15 (Original LP), 57:36 (2002 reissue)
Current edition: Sony/Columbia Legacy 2002 CD

In June 1967, Laura made her first major concert appearance, at the Monterey Pop Festival. At the invitation of organisers Lou Adler and John Phillips, she joined a legendary lineup that included Jefferson Airplane, Jimi Hendrix and Janis Joplin. Much has been written about the myth of Monterey. Taking to the stage in a black bat-winged dress with an under-rehearsed backing band and two members of the Hi Fashions, she cut an anomalous figure among the hippies and flower people of the 'Summer of Love' and came away convinced she'd been booed off stage. In fact, as close analysis of film of the event shows, that wasn't so. She'd misinterpreted the reaction, and so did others for years to come. Still, the damage was done to her confidence as a public performer. Lola Kirke, a singer-songwriter of a later generation, described to me how these false impressions can impact on an artist: 'I'm sure she had a lot of booing going on in her own head. And then as soon as you hear somebody booing you from out there, you're, like, 'OK, you're right. All the positive things I hear can't possibly be as correct as this one negative thing''.

Fortunately, Laura's recording career was now under way. Immediately after completing the first album, she started work on a second with the same team: Okun and Bernstein. Several new songs were recorded, including two that would appear on the eventual album: 'Sweet Blindness' and 'Stoned Soul Picnic'. But by then, she'd met David Geffen, a young agent for the William Morris

Agency with ambitions to be a media mogul. He found her a 'very strange girl', with hair 'down to her thighs' (he exaggerates), who wore purple lipstick and Christmas balls for earrings. But, as he told Joe Smith in a later interview, she was among the most talented people he'd ever seen in his life. He saw that in taking over her management, he could advance both her career and his own. They jointly formed Tuna Fish Music, Inc., a publishing company that would control all her copyrights. Having found a legal loophole in her current contract, he prised her away from Artie Mogull, then went in search of a new recording contract. Clive Davis – recently installed as president of Columbia Records – was looking to broaden the label's gene pool, and despite finding her appearance at Monterey 'amateurish and overdramatic', agreed to audition her. After complaining about the bright lighting in the audition room, she played for Davis by the glow of a TV set. He signed her – as he recalls in his autobiography – 'on the strength of her writing', and the hardheaded Geffen went on to negotiate a contract that gave Laura unprecedented creative control over her work.

The new team dumped the previous work and started recording the album afresh. Most sessions took place at night. Duties as arranger fell to Charlie Calello, a talented young staffer at Columbia who'd already worked with Lou Christie and The Four Seasons. When Laura first played him the material – by candlelight in her apartment – Calello says he was 'in tears'. She played the songs in exactly the sequence they appear on the finished album: evidence that she saw it as a 'concept album' (to use the then-fashionable jargon). When it came to his role as arranger, success depended on the intuitive partnership that developed between the two of them. She would give him vague indications of what she wanted a track to sound like (such as wanting it to be 'its own child') and leave him to make musical sense of her vision. Calello brought in a number of top New York session men to play on the album. Everything was performed live, with four or five horns and the rhythm section all in a 15 by 20 ft. room. As Calello recalled later to John Kruth, 'When she began to sing, everybody turned around to look at her, to get the feel'. Still limited to 4-track tape machines, he had to be creative in mixing and matching instrumental parts and vocal overdubs.

'The struggle in the city is between health and sickness: God and the Devil. That's been my experience', Laura told William Kloman in 1968, six months after the album's release. Her self-created world is peopled by larger-than-life characters: God, the Devil, someone she called 'The Captain'. Also present throughout is an inescapable theme of neediness, of dependence on a man, but dependence *on her own terms*. Patricia Romanowski wrote of Laura in *The Rolling Stone Book of Women in Rock*: 'She brought to the late-Sixties false utopia of guilt-free fucking a scalding dose of scintillating shame and delicious submission'.

The careful sequencing of tracks across the LP's two sides was Laura's, making for a concerted whole: a song cycle about a young woman's coming of age in the city. As if to underscore the point, the black-and-white image on the back cover shows on the right the silhouette of a woman, who appears to be Laura. Barely lit from a light source behind her, she kisses the forehead of another female figure in profile, who appears younger in age. In fact, it was a double exposure: both images are of Laura.

Nothing about *Eli and the Thirteenth Confession* was conventional. At Laura's insistence, the original US pressing used perfumed ink on the lyric sheet, which would later enable her college fans to identify each other by smelling its lingering aroma in each other's dorms. (When she discovered the factory had stopped adding the perfume, she complained to label boss Clive Davis. 'To keep Laura happy', as he puts it in his memoir, he instructed them to restart.)

She insisted on accompanying herself on piano, and the abrupt tempo changes and weird jazz voicings of her piano style were left unregulated. It would fall to others to make her songs hits, smoothing out their contours and simplifying the harmony; Laura stuck to her guns. The album credits were a declaration of intent: 'Laura Nyro: writer, composer, voices, piano and witness to the confession'. Pete Johnson's review for the *Los Angeles Times* was prophetic in declaring it 'one of the most stunning creations of recent pop music'. After the slightly uncertain start of her debut album, this was her first masterpiece. It wasn't immediately recognised as such – appreciation was slow to build – but its status is now assured.

'Luckie' (Laura Nyro)

The album opens in fighting mood. On a disc comprising 13 tracks, Laura begins by defying the superstition that the number 13 is unlucky. As we've seen, she had auditioned a song with the same title for Artie Mogull in 1966. While the earlier song shared a few lyrics with this one, now the ideas were incorporated into Laura's evolving secular theology. Where before luck had faced only 'trouble', her foe in the revised song is no less than the Devil himself. Fortunately, 'Luckie' – a personification of luck she carries inside her head – is taking over. She's 'ready for Luckie'. With his emblem of the lucky four-leaf clover, he's more than a match for the 'poor little Devil', who may be an 'artist of a sort' but is forced to take a 'back seat'.

This is the manifesto of a young woman determined to take control. One sign of that is there are several tempo changes – an acceleration at the words 'inside of my mind', and a slowing in the coda – respectfully observed in Calello's arrangement: just the sort of irregularity that Herb Bernstein would've smoothed out (and is ignored in the published sheet music). And in the album's carefully designed architecture, 'Luckie' – as the opener to side one – counterbalances the corresponding track on side two – 'Timer' – and the concluding (13th) track of the whole album, 'The Confession'.

'Lu' (Laura Nyro)

The air of exultation continues into the next track as Laura celebrates joyous submission to a man. He's in demand: everyone's calling him. The Devil has been driven back, at least temporarily, and the singer is walking 'on God's good side' with Luie. It would be crass to identify this character with any known boyfriend of Laura's at the time, though perhaps not irrelevant to recall that 'Louis' (usually shortened to 'Lou') was her father's name. Is the singer looking for a father figure? In the onrush of emotion, Laura, as ever, reaches for new words – drawing deep from a 'lovewell', she experiences her summer with Lu as a 'flameride'. Michele Kort suggests that Laura's varied reading might've taken her to the work of Gerard Manley Hopkins, the English Victorian poet renowned for coining neologisms of this sort: words like 'greenworld' and 'greybell'.

Musically, the track encapsulates Laura's eclecticism. It begins with a spare, laid-back jazz groove featuring some neat guitar fingerpicking. Charlie Calello has described how he'd play her something – for example, Art Blakey and The Jazz Messengers – saying 'Listen to the instrumentation: this is only trumpet and tenor sax'. She'd reply, 'Yeah, this would work'. 'The introduction to 'Lu' actually laid down the feeling of what she was going to do', Calello explains. But then, as we move into the chorus, she's in full girl-group mode – multitracking her voice to chant the man's name (think 'Jimmy Mack', the Motown classic she would cover on a later album). Then in a slower bridge section ('I will always be fair...'), she varies the approach again by ululating over the single syllable 'Lu'. It's a dazzling range of techniques to deploy in a single song of under three minutes.

'Sweet Blindness' (Laura Nyro)
Released as a single B-side, April 1968, b/w 'Eli's Comin'
Released as a single B-side, October 1968, b/w 'Stoned Soul Picnic'
With the 'Devil' banished (for now) and a man in her bed, the initial burst of youthful enthusiasm concludes with this celebration of the grape and the grain. Recorded on the same day as 'Luckie' and 'Lu', it forms the third panel of a kind of triptych. Calello understood these songs as 'impressionistic paintings of experiences' written from specific points of view. He suggests, "Sweet Blindness' was her actual definition of what it was like to get drunk; what it was like to be blind in a sense that it was sweet in a way that alcohol has a tendency to make you feel'. It may be a little more complicated than that. The lyric emphasises *illicit* drinking. The singer – perhaps underage – is consuming her 'daddy's wine'. She's not going to disclose what she's been drinking; he mustn't get to hear of it because 'He don't believe in the gin mill spirit'. The sense of intoxication is heightened, or sweetened, by the taste of bootlegged pleasure. Sex and alcohol seem to merge for Laura the 'moonshine lover'.

It's possible that Laura had been reading Emily Dickinson (1830-1886), one of the most anthologised of American poets. Dickinson's unflinchingly honest and psychologically penetrating verse would've struck a chord. The academic Patricia Spence Rudden has found similarities between 'Sweet Blindness' and Dickinson's short poem 'I Taste A Liquor Never Brewed'. Dickinson's poem uses the imagery of drinking to talk about her intoxication with nature. While Laura's song certainly involves alcohol, Rudden suggests its wider subject is the discovery of ecstasy – the rearrangement of the senses implicit in the phrase 'sweet blindness' – perhaps even a drug high, translated into the more acceptable language of legal drug use. Those who knew Laura say she wasn't a great alcohol drinker in youth; she preferred to smoke marijuana. One anecdote tells of her receiving a visit at home from the hard-drinking Janis Joplin, who left in a huff, complaining, 'You're no rock 'n' roller, you have no booze in the house!'.

The track barrels along in a lively arrangement, dominated by the brass section. As one of Laura's most accessible compositions, the song gained wider traction after The 5th Dimension released it as a single in September 1968 – a rather sloppy, burlesque version compared to the original that nevertheless reached number 13 in the *Billboard* chart. When later that year the group performed 'Sweet Blindness' on a TV special with a glittery-suited Frank Sinatra as guest member, Laura must have felt… well, what exactly? Best to return to the definitive version here.

'Poverty Train' (Laura Nyro)

If 'Sweet Blindness' was about the innocent pleasures of inebriation, the skies grow darker in 'Poverty Train'. The young protagonist has seen the underbelly of drug use. Although – perhaps in an effort to gain distance from the material – the reference is to 'getting off on sweet cocaine', she seems to be recalling a bad acid trip. During the personal experience, monsters – half-men, half-rats – filed into her room and menaced her from the walls. She found the strength to resist them, and after nine hours of spiritual combat, they withdrew. Silver light streamed into the room through the slats of the Venetian blinds as Laura fell asleep exhausted. She awoke the next day in a haze. As she described the experience to William Kloman in a 1968 *New York Times* interview, 'I won the struggle for myself. I stopped being a loser and became a winner instead'. It was, she told him, 'the day I became a woman'. Characteristically, the lyric recasts this decisive drug trip in theological and synaesthetic terms: she 'sees' the 'walls roar' as her brains 'become God', and she senses the Devil smiling at her. Drug users often describe addiction as like being on a train which you can board but never alight from – clearly, Laura was drawing on this imagery for her title here, as in a later song about hard drug use, 'Been On A Train'. This time, enticing as a trip may have looked in the opening verse, she's glad to get off the 'poverty train', and the song ends with the quietly sung single word 'Morning': it's over.

Appropriately, this is one of the album's most heartfelt tracks. An impassioned vocal soars over an arrangement that builds in girth from a lean beginning, before losing weight again. These outer sections are notionally in C minor, while the bulk of the song is in C major. But as always in Laura's music, tonality is ambiguous and chords are not readily classifiable; it was Calello's strength that he respected these idiosyncrasies. Joe Farrell's flute weaves memorable jazz arabesques around the voice, an effect Laura appreciated. She told *Downbeat* later: 'He kind of turned it into *Alice in Wonderland*, almost... he came into my world and he really enhanced it'. (Assuming she was referring to the children's classic and not the jazz standard of that name, it's an apt suggestion. The hippie generation often read Lewis Carroll's book as a kind of psychedelic road map.)

A blazing performance at the Monterey Festival in 1967 was captured on film. Director D. A. Pennebaker shot her in extreme close-up – you feel the song almost inscribed on her body and have to keep reminding yourself she was only 19 years old at the time. Afterwards, she thought the crowd were booing her. Not so – on the now cleaned-up audio, you clearly hear a woman shout 'Booo-tiful!'.

'Lonely Women' (Laura Nyro)

One day during recording, well-known jazz producer Jack Lewis dropped by the studio to hear what Laura was doing. When he heard 'Lonely Women', he urged Calello to bring in veteran tenor saxophonist Zoot Sims to play behind her. It was a good call. Sims – whose career stretched back to his time with The Woody Herman Big Band – hadn't recorded for several years, but the older man made an immediate impression on Laura, as she recalled in 1970:

> We played the tape for him. It was a rainy afternoon and the studio looked grey, this great big studio. Zoot Sims walked in with his head down to the floor, looking so down and everything. Then he did a thing with his sax where you just hear the air coming out and, like, it's all scratchy and broken and he communicates his loneliness into the song. Charlie and I sat there crying. It was so beautiful and it was so great because it was all in the air.

Sims' light airborne sax is the distinctive feature of this remarkable track. For much of the time, his is the only accompaniment to Laura's voice and piano. She sings the *blues* at several points by placing a D7 chord (containing an F#) under an F natural. In a faster breakout passage, the rhythm section kicks in as she sings the line, 'Don't got no children to be grandmother for'. Throughout, the lyric oscillates between first person and third: 'Let me die' and 'She don't believe no more'. Perhaps she's describing herself, perhaps everywoman, perhaps a composite character. Certainly, the 'Blues that make the walls rush in' return us to the previous track's terrifying hallucination. Whatever its origin, this is a stark vision of solitude or abandonment, from the same dark place as 'Poverty Train'.

'Eli's Comin'' (Laura Nyro)

Released as a single A-side, April 1968, b/w 'Sweet Blindness'
Released as a single B-side, June 1969, b/w 'Save The Country'
After a dark night of the soul (or two nights if we read autobiography into 'Lonely Women'), we're back in the daylight, as side one concludes with this

upbeat warning about a predatory male. Calello believes 'Eli's Comin'' was written about 'somebody that she was involved with'. There's no escaping this heartbreaker, it seems, hence the song's repeated line of advice to 'hide your heart, girl'. But even here, Laura translates what could be a little local romantic difficulty, onto a cosmic plane. Although she had no formal Jewish education, she may well have known that the name 'Eli' in Hebrew means 'My God'. And then there's this intriguing classical allusion: 'I walked to Apollo and the bay', she sings at one point. In Greek myth, the god Apollo pursues the mountain nymph Daphne, and in answer to her prayer for help, Mother Earth changes Apollo into a bay or laurel tree. The name 'Laura' derives from the Latin for bay laurel (The name 'Daphne', from the Greek, carries the same meaning). Since Apollo was the god of music, the song may be hinting not just at man trouble, but at an inevitable and ecstatic submission to the muse.

'Eli's Comin'' is one of two tracks where Laura doesn't play piano. Calello explained to her that he wanted to try a rhythmic device he'd used on a previous record, 'The Name Game' by Shirley Ellis. The idea was that the trombones play on beat 1 and the upbeat of 3 and the other horns play on 1 and 2 and the upbeat of 3. Laura, whose sense of rhythm was personal and idiosyncratic, felt she couldn't match that, so the producer transcribed her piano part and gave it to session man Paul Griffin. She then stood in front of the band and sang live (though the final take involved overdubs). After a slow intro, Laura's multitracked vocals build real excitement over a bright gospel rock bed with a vague sense of menace.

When 'Eli's Comin'' appeared as Laura's first single on the Columbia label, it attracted little attention. Once again, success came via a cover version. Three Dog Night were an American rock band fronted by three male vocalists. Their single version reached number 10 in the *Billboard* chart in November 1969 (in a week when there were also Nyro-penned songs at numbers 2 and 3). According to US surveys, the name 'Eli', which had fallen out of favour for male babies in earlier decades, came back into fashion in the early-1970s – perhaps an indirect consequence?

'Timer' (Laura Nyro)
Released as a single B-side, June 1968, b/w 'Save The Country'

At this time, Laura was living on the Upper West Side. Her live-in companions in the Manhattan apartment were a German shepherd, Beautybelle, and a black cat called Timer. When Laura was on trips away, the dog got to accompany her while Timer was boarded out. In concert, she'd say (mischievously) that this song was about her cat. But Laura's early songs are rarely so straightforward. Interviewed by John Stix years later, Calello understood the lyric as referring to the inevitability of ageing: 'One day you're going to look at yourself and you're not going to know where it happened'. In that sense, it's of a piece with the precocious intimation of mortality in 'And When I Die'. Calello even takes credit for one line: Laura sings, 'You're a jigsaw, Timer'. Calello said to her, 'Isn't it God that is the jigsaw?'. Laura agreed, perhaps sensing a way to incorporate the song into her secular theology, and added the line 'God is a jigsaw'. The meaning is perhaps that the cosmic picture is larger than we can comprehend, unless, and until, all the pieces are fitted together.

In the song, time personified is seen as an ineluctable force, rocking the singer's cradle as an infant, changing her face as she grows up. It whips up a storm, but the storm will pass ('Let it blow') and time(r) knows 'The lady's gonna love again'. She's walking forward with the 'master of time', yet also looking back, nostalgic for a time when she didn't know about money and could walk through the 'gates of space' onto a 'pleasure ground'.

Placed significantly at the start of side two – after the enforced pause as the listener flipped the disc over – this is one of Laura's most cryptic lyrics, but is conveyed with an engaging range of vocal techniques. As usual, tempo shifts accompany mood shifts in the lyric: she starts at around 84 bpm, accelerating to 100 by the seventh bar ('she got up'). The line 'Let it blow' is delivered with a positively operatic roulade, skittering down a two-octave scale, while at mention of the 'cradle', her backing vocals take on a little-girl innocence. A mini-drama in under three and a half minutes.

'Stoned Soul Picnic' (Laura Nyro)
Released as a single A-side, October 1968, b/w 'Sweet Blindness'
And so to one of Laura's most celebrated songs. After the complexities of 'Timer', it's a song to parallel 'Sweet Blindness' from side one and is a celebration of straightforward intoxication. Earlier themes are picked up – 'time and wine' – but this picnic offers other pleasures besides: the chance to get 'stoned'. We know Laura was a liberal cannabis user at the time (Calello was anxious when she brought joints into recording sessions). It's possible that – in another back-reference – by pivoting on a pun, she's hinting at a benign, 'soft' side of drugs. They don't take you on a 'poverty train' – instead, narcotics promise 'trains' of blossoms, of music, of trust, of thought. The lyric is wonderfully concentrated in this respect. How many meanings are wrapped up in the phrase 'sassafras and moonshine'! Sassafras is a hallucinogen that promotes feelings of empathy and closeness. The plant it derives from is a member of the laurel family (another pun on her own name?). 'Moonshine' is both beguiling light and – in the sense of bootleg liquor – an ambiguous nod to the earlier track. Some promoters took the song's invitation literally. The *Los Angeles Free Press* of 27 September 1968 carried an advert from a record store on Santa Monica Boulevard:

Music Revolution invites you to a stoned soul picnic in honour of Laura Nyro this Saturday 12 noon at Griffith Park, Ferndell Picnic Area.

We can assume that illicit substances were consumed on that occasion.

Driven by piano and congas, the syncopated hook that underpins the track is irresistible. Although similar in some ways to the Afro-Cuban groove of The

Young Rascals' 'Groovin'' – a number-1 hit in 1967 that would surely have come Laura's way – she makes of it a signature rhythm. (The fact that The Young Rascals' leader, Felix Cavaliere, would go on to produce her later album *Christmas and the Beads of Sweat* provides another point of connection.)

'*Surry* down to a stoned soul picnic'. Generations have puzzled over this line. Some people have heard 'surrey', as in the horse-drawn vehicle memorialised in Rodgers and Hammerstein's 'The Surrey With The Fringe On Top'. I find this an unlikely mode of transport for a hippie be-in (although it's true that when recording her next album, she'd travel to the sessions in a horse-drawn carriage through Central Park). Another suggestion is that 'surry' is a shortening of 'Let's hurry'. Personally, I hear 'scurry' with one consonant removed, or perhaps slower forms of travel with a hissing sibilant at the start: words like 'saunter' or 'sashay'. When Calello asked what the word meant, Laura prevaricated: 'Oh, it's just a nice word'. The fact is that sometimes she simply made words up. Humpty Dumpty tells Lewis Carroll's Alice that words mean whatever he chooses them to mean – this seemed to be Laura's position likewise; and, once out in the world, they mean whatever *we* want them to mean. As she repeats the now-familiar word over the fade-out, extending the second syllable into an endless diphthong, it becomes almost an incantation.

Bones Howe, producer of The 5th Dimension, got hold of an acetate of Laura performing 'Stoned Soul Picnic' and immediately spotted a potential hit for his own protégés. Their single (a much more relaxed treatment – less joyful, more literal – released in June 1968) peaked at 3 on the *Billboard* chart. In a story so often repeated, Laura's own version failed to chart when issued as a single later in the year.

One creative artist's response to the song is worth dwelling on. Writers on Laura repeatedly quote Broadway maestro Stephen Sondheim saying of 'Stoned Soul Picnic' that 'The song's complexity, economy and spontaneity sum up for him what music is all about'. The line derives from a 1968 profile of Laura in the *New York Times*. It's a striking quote because, although Sondheim remained aware of music that surrounded him – like the singer-songwriter movement of the 1960s – he was always a theatre writer with little interest in songs unconnected to musicals. However, he made an exception for Laura. 'A genius, pure and simple, a genius', he called her in an interview with the *Boston Globe* in March 1970. Likewise, speaking to the *Los Angeles Times* in October 1971: 'Most rock I find boring: simple in the wrong way, meaning dull. I've enjoyed a lot of The Beatles' stuff and some really brilliant things by Laura Nyro'.

Sheila Weller's study of Laura's contemporaries, *Girls Like Us*, includes another Sondheim quote about 'Stoned Soul Picnic' (albeit unsourced): 'In economy, lyricism and melody, it is a masterpiece'. Shortly before his death in 2021, I had a chance to put Weller's line to the great man himself and received a brusque response: 'I never said any such thing. 'Masterpiece' is a word I use very rarely. *Where did you read that?*'. These two musical giants – Sondheim and Nyro – only met on one occasion: in 1969, an event captured in memorable photos by Stephen Paley. 'It was a very slight acquaintance', Sondheim told me 50 years later, 'One afternoon and one dinner'. Paley remembers it rather differently: as 'a big love fest'. The elderly titan may have downplayed his enthusiasm in retrospect, but it's clear that the young Sondheim responded to the inherent theatricality in Laura's work.

'Emmie' (Laura Nyro)
Hitherto, all Laura's love songs, however unconventional in form, had been about man trouble. 'Emmie' was a first early clue to her bisexuality. Although it could be read as a *character* song in which Laura, in male guise, addresses a female lover, its intensity and intimacy point us elsewhere. According to Geffen, it was written for Laura's journalist friend Ellen Sander: a suggestion that Laura herself didn't entirely deny when put to her. The two women were close, but the relationship, according to Sander, was not sexual. Safer to say that the song wraps up Laura's feelings for a number of women she was close to, its open-endedness allowing future generations of lesbian and bisexual women to recognise themselves in its carefully honed lines. Years later, in an interview with Paul Zollo for *SongTalk*, she said the song was addressed to 'the eternal feminine'. Certainly, when she sings the line 'Time to design a woman', it sounds like a declaration of intent: from here on, the remaining tracks of the album – the time remaining, as it were – will be used to outline the 'eternal feminine'.

Laura could sometimes be obscure, but at other times a line of lucid simplicity jumps out at you, like this one: 'Emily, you ornament the earth/For me'. By identifying Emmie with natural forces (the snow, the 'unstudied sea'), she may again be thinking of another Emily: Emily Dickinson, whose poetry regularly projected human emotion onto the world around her.

'Laura was a true romantic, and understood the importance of passion and sensuality', her friend Madeline Sunshine recalls: 'Lit candles and perfume were staples in her apartment'.

This track certainly gets the most *romantic* arrangement on the album, complete with vibes, strings and harp *glissandi*. The piano is low in the mix until the final verse ('Your mama's been a-callin' you'), where Laura's vocal grows more strident – leading to the final repeated line, 'She got the way to move me, Emmie', incorporating a perhaps unconscious lift from Neil Diamond's 'Cherry Cherry' released two years earlier. The change of tone jars slightly but is characteristic of her style at the time; ever restless, her music rarely settles for long in one groove. When she returned to the song in the late-1980s (a performance captured on *Live at the Bottom Line*), she replaced this repeated coda with a list of female archetypes: Mother, Daughter, Sister, Lover.

'Woman's Blues' (Laura Nyro)
From the specific to the general, from 'Emmie' to 'Woman'. This somewhat frantic tirade is one of the less convincing cuts on an album where the quality

rarely dips. It opens with a beautiful slow chorale for the brass: one of Calello's most inspired contributions to the album. Laura is describing the promise of joy at the outset of a relationship. After that, however, the tempo quickens and the meter shifts from a loose 12/8 to a standard rock 4/4 as the rhythm section kicks in – and something is lost. Somehow the singer's usual articulacy deserts her as she vents her spleen against a man who has now run off, leaving her 'motherless' (a curious notion). She was immured 'on the chamber's walls of heartache', and now she's 'got to get gone'. At one point, she parodies the playground rhyme, 'One, two, three, four, five, six, seven/All good children go to heaven': Laura's ex is warned he'll 'never get to heaven'. Finally, she cuts herself free, with the curse 'And damn be done'.

With its references to God and heaven, the song unfolds against the same cosmic backdrop as the other tracks, yet seems less considered. Perhaps that's why it has attracted few other artists. An exception is Brooklyn-born slam poet Dana Bryant, whose version on a 1997 tribute album evacuated the melody altogether as she rapped the lyrics to the accompaniment of a scratching turntablist.

'Once It Was Alright Now (Farmer Joe)' (Laura Nyro)

Here comes another teasing lyric. We seem to be given the beginning and end of a story and left to fill in the missing pieces. The setting is small-town America, or rural America, or somewhere in between. It's a place with cornfields and a 'town shoemaker', a folksy world of train whistles and farm workers. The singer is running from a violent relationship: be afraid, this man has a gun. With typical evasion of perspective, Laura moves between a third-person narrator ('She said…') and a first-person speaker ('I've got to see about a man I know'). Of course, the latter could be heard as direct speech *reported* by the narrator, although the printed lyrics make no use of quotation marks, so it remains unclear just who is who. It seems unlikely this farmer is the same 'Joe' she was taking leave of in 'Goodbye Joe': this has more the feel of pictorial invention.

However cryptic the lyrics, Laura compensates by acting out the story with her voice. Meaning is created at the intersection between music and language. The insistent repetition of the word 'run' over two lines, emphasises the quickening pace of events. When she sings 'Fire', we imagine the gunshot; the next line ('flames of gold…') is gabbled, evoking her panic. In all, there must be half a dozen tempo changes here, not to mention a temporary key change from F to E, dislocating the listener in a way no three-minute pop song should. The effect is not unlike rapid cuts in cinema.

As with 'Eli's Comin'', Laura left keyboard duties on this track to Paul Griffin, whose hard-driving blues rock piano underpins the arrangement.

'December's Boudoir' (Laura Nyro)

After venturing out on the narrative road and seeming to depart from her confining self in the previous song, Laura returns to her intimate space:

this is song as pillow talk. We're in her 'boudoir': a sensuous, comforting environment, a safe space. Baby, it's cold outside, but inside she's warmed by the 'flames of December'. After the catalogue of no-hope lovers in previous songs, she welcomes kisses that are 'true'. This time she knows who her lover is. Earlier themes return in new guise. Where previously time had seemed threatening, now she feels 'ageless', capable of loving 'timelessly'. Emily's love had been 'Carved in a heart on a berry tree'; now, that tree is recalled in a neologism, as 'Decemberry ice' – the image, perhaps, of red holly berries standing out against white snow. In a feast for the senses, the song also evokes taste and smell with references to melons, spices and marzipan.

Much of this is sung in a breathy, feline tone, close to the microphone, Laura's piano supported discreetly by woodwinds, strings and harp. The melody never heads in predictable directions. You'd say she was improvising, were her deportment not so controlled. Those with a technical turn of mind should seek online the work of scholar Levent Donat Berköz, who has analysed this song's harmonic structure and shows it to be daunting in its complexity, right down to the final chord: an unusual GmMAJ7. Laura was not a highly trained musician, but intuitively she pushed at the limits of the popular music vocabulary. In its expressive sophistication, 'December's Boudoir' looks forward to 'Gibsom Street', a highlight of her next album – but there the subject matter will be very different.

'The Confession' (Laura Nyro)

Interviewed by the *Los Angeles Herald-Examiner* in 1968, Laura said: 'I had just finished with a man, and knew I had to write this song about it. It had to be, you know, joyful. I didn't know what the notes would be, but I knew what they'd sound like'. Many of the album's earlier songs had been about *finishing* a relationship. As her biographer suggests, what she seems to allude to here is a happier kind of finish: the release of orgasm. For her listeners, the invitation to 'super ride inside my lovething' was an unusually explicit proposal to hear from a female recording artist in 1968. Of course, pop and rock had always been about sex, but here Laura wrestles ownership of the subject back from swaggering phallic rock gods – those boys with guitars slung low over their crotches – to present the *female* experience. This is her 'confession'. Empowered, ready to admit she'd had previous lovers, she realises she was 'born a woman/Not a slave'. Curiously, at the very point of sexual fulfilment, she feels reborn as a 'virgin', and, in the final lines of this final track, the secular and theological collide for the last time – she first directs attention downwards to her 'lovething', then lifts her gaze upwards to conclude that 'Love is surely gospel'. She told Michael Thomas of *Eye* magazine that she'd thought a couple of times of becoming a nun, but the snag was her liking for men: 'I like God and men. But I have to have both'. Like Aretha Franklin and many another soul sister, Laura repurposes the language of gospel music, substituting – or perhaps supplementing – God with someone more beddable.

A striking feature of the album's lyrics is how she repeatedly refers to 'Mama' and 'Daddy'. It would be a crass interpreter who identified these figures with Laura's own parents – very much alive at the time – especially as 'Daddy' in 'The Confession' offers wise counsel 'thru his grave'. Perhaps we should see them rather as ancestor figures, part of a cast of archetypes that also includes God and the Devil.

Musically, this may be the album's *straightest* track. Without significant tempo changes, it powers forward, steered by rhythm guitar rather than piano. Very different from the sinuous 'December's Boudoir', the verse melody simply repeats, reaching a crescendo on the line 'I confess!'. Appropriate to an outpouring of joy – appropriate to an evocation of coitus, if such is intended – the track makes a fitting finale to a 46-minute personal odyssey.

2002 Bonus Tracks
'Lu (Demo)', 'Stoned Soul Picnic (Demo)', 'Emmie (Demo)'
(Laura Nyro)

These three demos were all recorded on 29 November 1967. On 'Lu', the harmonies are slightly different in the opening lines, but otherwise, it sounds much like a template for the orchestrated end result. On 'Stoned Soul Picnic', which has elementary vocal overdubs, we hear how her backing vocals were integral to the original conception. In Laura's original manuscript lyric of 'Emmie', as reproduced in *Lyrics and Reminiscences*, the final verse appears as 'You are my friend/And I love you'. By the time she demo'd the song, the present tenses had become past tenses: 'You *were* my friend', etc. Laura-the-songwriter was distancing herself from whatever was going on in Laura-the-woman's life.

Calello has said that the entire album exists in demo form, all recorded in a single day. If that is so, the remaining tracks have yet to emerge from the archives.

New York Tendaberry (1969)

Personnel:
Laura Nyro: vocals, piano
Gary Chester: drums
Bob Bushwell: bass
Bernie Glow, Lew Soloff: trumpet
Jimmie Haskell: conductor, orchestral arranger
Recorded at Columbia Studios, New York City, September 1968-July 1969
Producers: Roy Halee, Laura Nyro
Engineer: Roy Halee
Label: Columbia
Release date: 24 September 1969 (US), January 1970 (UK)
Chart place: US: 32
Running time: 46:15 (Original LP), 51:06 (2002 reissue)
Current edition: Sony/Columbia Legacy 2002 CD

'It's scandalous that there's no book on Laura Nyro. One could write a book on *New York Tendaberry* alone'. Thus wrote music critic Ian MacDonald in *Uncut* in 2000. It was certainly her most adventurous album to date and repays close scrutiny and endless listening. For many, this is her masterpiece. For me, it's a close-run contest with *Eli*. But in the torrent of late-decade innovation that followed The Beach Boys' *Pet Sounds* (1966) and The Beatles' *Sgt. Pepper's Lonely Hearts Club Band* (1967), *Tendaberry* is another sky-high achievement.

Charlie Calello was not in the producer's chair this time. It's not entirely clear why. He later told interviewer John Stix that Columbia's new head of A&R fired him because he'd spent way over budget in making *Eli* (a total of about $45,000, more than double the average production cost at the time). A different version, reported by Michele Kort, is that he felt Laura's new songs needed more work and she was no longer willing to listen to his advice. Whatever the reason, David Geffen went in search of a new producer and, with Laura's approval, alighted on his friend Roy Halee. Halee, whose credits stretched back to Bob Dylan's early work, was impressed – if daunted – by her perfectionism in the studio.

Work began in October 1968. After they junked an early attempt to record live with a band – Laura's musical time-keeping, her taste for the varying tempo known as *rubato*, was always a challenge to session men – Halee focused on creating the best possible vocal/piano track as a basis for elaboration. It was a painstaking process. Laura would spend hours in a darkened studio, recording fragments of songs. When she realised she wasn't feeling a particular song, she'd simply go on to the next. The initial results were fragments that only she could assemble. But by late spring 1969, she was ready to add orchestration. Her first choice of collaborator was Gil Evans, the arranger on Miles Davis' greatest albums, but he didn't respond to her letter. Halee then suggested Jimmie Haskell. Laura admired Haskell's work on Simon & Garfunkel's 'Old

Friends'; even more, his work with Bobbie Gentry, which made for a good fit. As Laura told Chris Albertson at the time: 'I know that he's *there* already, because on Bobbie Gentry's album, he creates the delta, and it's syrupy, and you can almost hear the crickets and bugs'.

Laura didn't read or write musical notation. She'd sing parts to Haskell and he would transcribe them. She heard music as colours, and it was up to fellow musicians to grasp her personal language. Thus she might ask Haskell for 'light blue' in one place and 'pink' somewhere else. As he explained later to David Fricke: 'I interpreted light blue as middle-to-high instruments, playing softly. Pink would be those instruments playing louder. If she went up to white, it was the loudest, brassiest sound I could think of'. A 'blue' instrument could be a viola; a 'brown' instrument something like a bass clarinet, she agreed. For all their challenges, he remembers these recording sessions with fondness. She'd dress for the occasion, with her characteristically flamboyant dress sense, and each evening she'd have dinner brought in, which they ate by candlelight. Word was getting out that mighty work was afoot. Visitors to the studio included Liza Minnelli, and on one occasion Miles Davis. Laura boldly asked her hero if he'd play on the album. 'I can't play on this', he said, 'You did it already'. (In June 1970, Davis and his Quartet would play four nights at the Fillmore East, New York City, as Laura's support act: a neat turn of events.)

By now, the studio was using 16-track machines. This greatly enhanced the possibilities for mixing and overdubbing. But, by multiplying the choices available to artist and producer, it also dragged out the recording process. Halee was working simultaneously on Simon & Garfunkel's *Bridge over Troubled Water* and was under pressure to finish both projects. When Laura finally delivered her album to Columbia in September 1969 after more than nine months' gestation, friends sent her cards saying, 'Congratulations on your birth'. What's notable, considering the resources poured into it, is how spare the album sounds. Haskell's arrangements are far more reticent than Calello's. There's a lot of space, most of it filled by Laura and her piano alone. Rather like Joni Mitchell's *Blue* (1971) – which *Tendaberry* surely influenced – this is a music of intense subjectivity, such as had rarely been heard in rock or pop hitherto. As the centrepiece of a trilogy, it's her deepest act of self-exploration. In David Gahr's cover photo, she looks upwards, eyes closed, as if deep in reverie. Those who cultivate privacy inevitably invite prying eyes, and Laura took refuge in obliqueness and metaphor: it should come as no surprise if the lyrics and music prove resistant to interpretation.

For all its supposed difficulty, the response was stronger to this album than to its predecessor. An initial pressing of 150,000 copies sold out quickly. Laura was developing a cult following. Critics, too, were catching up, with fewer complaints of shrillness and more plaudits for her blend of sensuality and moral fervour. Reviewing her own work for the 1997 compilation *Stoned Soul Picnic*, Laura wept when she heard the album again, drawn back after 30 years to what she called its 'madcap energy'.

'You Don't Love Me When I Cry' (Laura Nyro)

The album opens with a new level of confidence – confidence in one's own powers, and courage. The opening line is Laura at her most enigmatic: 'Two mainstream die'. What could it mean? It's possible she intends to refer us back to a similarly obscure phrase in 'December's Boudoir': 'Mainstream marzipan sweet'. Whatever was sweet before has now turned to bitterness and gall.

It's a slow song, harmonically unpredictable, rendered in the simplest of arrangements. For much of the track, we're conscious only of Laura's voice and piano. Details like the delicate guitar arpeggios added in the second verse only direct attention back to the voice. She deploys the full range of her vocal techniques here: that confidence again! Beginning from a soft whisper, she rapidly jacks up the volume and intensity to hit the critical word 'goodbye'. Is she crying or screaming? Notice how – like the blues singers she admired – she slides up from G natural to G# on the word 'Mister' ('Mister I got funky blues'), as if to suggest the slipperiness of whatever bozo she's addressing in this aria of disillusionment, then holds on for *so* long to the word 'blues', before allowing the sound to tail away. Between verses, there's a silence, a dramatic pause. Few rock artists had dared to use silence, or to create such spacious arrangements; she has learnt that less is more. The only weakness here, to my mind, is the fade-out over a piano vamp, which seems a rather conventional conclusion to such an *un*conventional track.

'Captain For Dark Mornings' (Laura Nyro)

Like the true dramatist that she was, Laura saw the need to structure the album from sharp contrasts. This second track could hardly be more different from what's gone before. It's the first of the album's *character* songs. We meet the 'soft and silly' Lillianaloo – daughter of a gambling father, who's had bad experiences at the hands of sailors, tailors and soldiers, but now has found *the one*, her 'captain', for whom she's prepared to lay down her life. It's a celebration of heroic submission to a dream lover. Those who knew Laura at the time suggest she was always looking for that love supreme, a 'captain'. By turning the quest into a whimsical fable, as here, she distances herself from the material and universalises it. She'll give romance a different twist in the corresponding song on side two, 'Captain Saint Lucifer'.

Between verses, instead of the one-bar silence of 'You Don't Love Me When I Cry', we get an unexpected outburst of brass. But otherwise, this is another sparse arrangement, leaving room – at points where lyrics give way to mere vowel sounds – for Laura's sensuous vocalising. Here, unlike the previous track, the repeat-and-fade is very gradual, as she sings 'Captain say yes', drawing out the final sibilant – an erotic invitation male and female listeners alike can identify with, whether as the one issuing the invitation or the one receiving it.

There may be faint, no more than faint, echoes of 19th-century poet Walt Whitman in her call for a 'fearless captain'. Most American schoolchildren would've been exposed to Whitman's eulogy for the dead Abraham Lincoln that begins, 'O Captain! my Captain! our fearful trip is done/The ship has weather'd every rack, the prize we sought is won'. If this echo was intentional, it makes a connection to the political assassinations that prompted a later track on the album, 'Save The Country'. Certainly, the phrase 'fearless captain' (followed by the next line beginning with the word 'Die') calls forth the most strident delivery, on a track where the voice dynamics again range from *piano* to *forte*.

This was the track Joni Mitchell selected as one of her own top 12 in a programme for BBC Radio in 1983. 'She's got so much dynamic range and sense of theatre and composition. She's a great one', was the Canadian's verdict on her American contemporary.

'Tom Cat Goodbye' (Laura Nyro)

Laura's friends have suggested that this song is about her first real boyfriend, a man named Tom, who had the wandering habits of a tomcat. If so, he has disappeared into the realms of storybook. The dark-haired Laura here transforms herself into the blowsy blonde Rosie Pearl, who has borne Tom Cat's children but waits in vain for him to return at night. Invoking a story within the story, Rosie Pearl admires the example of Frankie and Johnny. In the traditional song – of which over 250 recordings have been made – Frankie finds her man, Johnny, making love to another woman and shoots him dead. Rosie Pearl reckons she'd have done the same to her two-timing husband.

Structurally, the song is worlds away from the simple ballad form of 'Frankie And Johnny'. After a slow narrative introduction, we go into a fast section in cut common time, as Rosie Pearl vents her rage. The tempo then slows down again for a triple-time segment. Curiously, the lines sung here are not included in the lyrics as printed. (They appear in the 1971 sheet music edition but may not be accurately transcribed: the edition has 'gonna find me, and...' where Laura appears to sing 'gonna buy me land'.) These later lines reveal Tom Cat as a failed aspirant to the movie business: 'You know you're never gonna make a moviemaker/ Always be a city faker'. Now Rosie Pearl grows more determined. She's going to the country 'to kill my lover man'. As the song zigzags through several more tempo changes, Laura acts out the increasingly frenzied part she has created for her character. Love her or loathe her – inspired tragedienne or wailing banshee – this is the intense performer that listeners recognise as having little parallel in the music of her time.

'Mercy On Broadway' (Laura Nyro)

Another character song. This time, the heroine is a young aspiring singer named Madison, who confronts the realities of the music (or musical theatre) business. If Tom Cat's creative ambitions are rightly going nowhere, Madison is a victim of what Joni Mitchell would later call 'the star-maker machinery behind the popular song'. Madison finds, 'There ain't no mercy now/On Broadway'.

Beyond that observation, it's hard to discern what's going on in this dense lyric, which characteristically fluctuates between the first- and third-person. Broadway is personified as a merciless female who'll 'make you pay' – perhaps. Madison once enjoyed a 'sweet July' of success before 'doom swept the band away' – perhaps. The song remains pregnant with possibilities, though the conclusion is surely defiant – repeated calls for everybody to 'shine', then a final contemptuous 'Ha!' over an open C doubled in octaves on the piano.

She wanted what she called a 'collage' of city noises on the track. In a profile for *Life* magazine, Maggie Paley recalls Laura coming into the control room during sessions to play with the different kinds of bells and chimes she'd bought that morning. This feature isn't much in evidence in the final mix, although – perhaps in homage to the section of Broadway known as The Great White Way – it's a bigger production than other cuts on the album, with much more use of multitracked vocals. Most strikingly, a gunshot sound effect interrupts the line 'There ain't no mercy now': Rosie Pearl may have settled scores in the country, but the city is a far more violent place. Just how murderously violent will be manifest in the next track.

'Save The Country' (Laura Nyro)

Released as a single A-side, January 1970, b/w 'New York Tendaberry'

In the early morning of 5 June 1968, presidential candidate Robert F. Kennedy was mortally wounded at the hands of gunman Sirhan Sirhan in a Los Angeles hotel. He died the following day. The death, coming just two months after the assassination of Martin Luther King, Jr. in Memphis, Tennessee, shook the nation and affected Laura deeply. The result, written at speed, was her most overtly political song to date.

Her first stab at the track was released as a single, a misfiring attempt at chart success (see below). Dissatisfied, she re-recorded the song for the *Tendaberry* album. The lyric brings together the communal fervour of the gospel tradition, the idealism of the peace movement and the single-mindedness of civil rights activism. As well as references to the 'glory river' and riding the 'dove' of peace, she quotes two rallying cries of the era: 'We shall overcome' and 'I can't study war no more' (a variation of the line 'Ain't gonna study war no more' from the spiritual 'Down By The Riverside'). The song clearly links the assassinations of Robert and John F. Kennedy (the 'two young brothers') with that of Dr. King (the 'king at the glory river').

The album version, which closes side one, is taken slower than the single, at least until the frantic finale. Up till then, it's just Laura and her strident, syncopated piano-playing. At the cry of 'Save the people', a tight brass section kicks in. The recording session was gruelling, and Laura called on friend Lew Soloff – trumpet player with Blood, Sweat & Tears – to help out the sidemen, who'd grown fatigued.

An early live performance has been caught on film. This was one of the two numbers ('He's A Runner' was the other) she sang on Bobby Darin's TV special

Kraft Music Hall: Sound of the Sixties in 1969. Remarkably, she produces the same energy level as on the recording, ending with a manic yelp of 'Now!'. A few months earlier, she'd told journalist William Kloman: 'The real United States of America is about to be born. That's what's coming out of the revolution'. In the years since, the song has become something of an American anthem at moments of national upheaval, a clarion call for healing in times of division. When rioters invaded the US Capitol in January 2021 seeking to overturn the result of the Presidential election, one of the popular memes circulating on the internet had a soundtrack of Laura's recording of 'Save The Country'.

In later life she was reluctant to revisit the song or answer questions about it. On a rare occasion at the Bottom Line, NYC, in 1993, she dusted it down but replaced the climactic 'Save the country now!' with some emollient lines from 'Stoned Soul Picnic': the angry young woman had given way to a calmer older self, the fury in her soul now assuaged. As she told interviewer Richard Knight, Jr. in 1994, this now represented her 'philosophy in a nutshell'. Later she would write many issues-based songs. Somehow the one undoubted protest song of her early career didn't seem to fit anymore.

'Save The Country' has been covered many times – by The 5th Dimension (inevitably) and (more thoughtfully) by Julie Driscoll with Brian Auger and the Trinity, Thelma Houston, and (on a recent tribute album) Shawn Colvin. When arch-rapper Kanye West sampled Laura's original on his 2007 album *Graduation*, he sped it up almost beyond recognition: this was not respectful.

'Gibsom Street' (Laura Nyro)

Side one opened with the melancholy of 'You Don't Love Me When I Cry'. Turn the disc over, and the corresponding position on side two is occupied by this bleak masterpiece, one of the most extraordinary things Laura ever committed to vinyl. Speaking to *Newsweek* in July 1969 as she wrapped up the recording, Laura observed: 'The gutter is a nasty, pitiful place for a woman. It's a lack of meaning, of dignity, of freedom. Once you've cleaned your soul one time, it's easy. But it's like cleaning house. You can't do it just once'.

Gibsom Street is a fictional location in New York City, where the 'Devil' is hungry for new victims; he has eyes for the vulnerable and exploits their weaknesses. The atmosphere of barely lit menace is deftly suggested by the line 'They hang the alley cats on Gibsom Street'. By implication, this is the hangout of back-street abortionists, and the singer has gone there, wishing the baby she carries were 'forbidden', and wishing to keep her 'mirror hidden'. (In traditional Jewish practice, it's customary to cover the mirrors when a household is in mourning.) The last verse may allude to the man who got her pregnant, who gave her the 'strawberry' that she sucked, unknowing of the consequences. It has been suggested there may be an echo of Laura's poetry reading here. In 'Goblin Market', a narrative poem by Christina Rossetti (1830-1894), the heroine – named Laura – is seduced by the calls of 'goblin' merchants who sell their fantastical fruits by the river. She gorges on the juices, but when she tells her sister of the pleasure they've given, the sister reminds her of another girl who partook of the forbidden fruit and died.

If the metaphors in 'Gibsom Street' are tightly packed, the musical language is disjunct rhetoric, nearer to modern jazz than rock 'n' roll. The piano introduction is unusually long – a slow, brooding vamp, nominally in her favourite key of C, but as harmonically erratic as anything she conceived. The voice enters, at first with quiet advice, growing louder, anguished at the thought of the Devil's handiwork. Tension rises, and the cry 'No more sorrow, no more moanin'' is a cue to unleash the brass ensemble. In a 1970 interview with *Life* magazine's Maggie Paley, Laura explained her intention here:

My first session with them, I had about twelve horns in the middle... They were playing it very clean, and I wanted it to be overemotional, so I got an idea. I said to them, 'Now when you play it, make believe you're Indians on the warpath', because that fit the music and the feeling I wanted. And then they looked at each other: Indians? On the warpath? And they played like Indians on the warpath, and I got what I wanted.

'Time And Love' (Laura Nyro)
Released as a single A-side, October 1969, b/w 'The Man Who Sends Me Home'

The last track left the singer sleeping on the ill-fated Gibsom Street 'across the river'. Now the mood lifts. Winter has frozen the river, but 'time is gonna bring you spring'. As the seasons turn and the weather improves, we shouldn't be fooled by the Devil; rather, draw inspiration from his adversary Jesus, who gave his life 'so sacred bells could sing'. Time is a great healer. Love conquers all. It's a familiar message – somewhat banal, particularly when this normally inventive lyricist rhymes 'love' with 'dove' (not for the first, or last, time). The middle eight breaks some new ground, however – in a signal of Laura's emerging social consciousness, she insists that woman, regardless of ethnicity, is a 'fighter'.

Life's Maggie Paley was privileged to watch Laura laying down the harmony tracks to 'Time And Love'. Dressed in a long black jumpsuit, having turned off all the lights in the recording room, Laura 'danced and paced and frowned as she alternately sang and listened to playbacks, embroidering sound over sound until it felt right to her'.

The music follows a conventional pop structure, even down to its sing-along chorus. It's no surprise that other artists fell on this one (where few have dared to tackle 'Gibsom Street'). There are respectable cover versions by Diana Ross, Barbra Streisand and much-loved British songbird Petula Clark, among others.

This optimistic and buoyant song predates other material on *Tendaberry*. Laura copyrighted it as early as 1966, and it was one of those recorded in 1967 with Okun and Bernstein for the aborted Verve follow-up to her first album. Evidently, she felt it better to hold it over. As light relief between the heavier tracks that flank it, its positioning here is surely by design.

'The Man Who Sends Me Home' (Laura Nyro)

Released as a single B-side, October 1969, b/w 'Time And Love'
The inside booklet of *Tendaberry* featured Stephen Paley's photo of the view
from Laura's apartment at 145 W. 79th Street. We're looking out over a rain-
soaked terrace at the New York skyline. Lights are on, it's late afternoon or
early evening. The photo seems to correspond to the mood of this compact
little love song. One touch of her man raises her to 'rooftops in his eyes',
she sings. One imagines a passionate relationship, vertiginous in intensity,
conducted high above street level. Inspiration for the song may have come
from her romance at the time with Jim Fielder, bass player for Blood, Sweat
& Tears. Another of Paley's photographs, which was later used in the 1971
songbook, shows Laura with Fielder on the terrace, a discarded teddy bear at
her feet. His face obscured, he clasps her legs while she appears to look out
over the city. It's the perfect visual analogue for the album's themes.

The lyric here speaks of a willing submission, but not of docility. This
is a woman of strength, as she reminds us with the strident piano chords
that interrupt the quiet reverie. Again, Haskell's contribution – wispy
ornamentation from woodwinds, for the most part – is reticent to the point of
disappearing altogether.

'Sweet Lovin' Baby' (Laura Nyro)

The topic of submission to a lover is continued in the next song. The singer
'belong(s)' to her man. When the bed is empty, she knows loneliness. The
central section of the lyric veers off into anecdote, although the meaning is
teasingly opaque. Laura was, to quote the Bard, a 'snapper-up of unconsidered
trifles'. Words or phrases would enter her sensorium and lodge there a while,
to reappear spun with her own meaning.

Apparently, Donald Boudreau, Laura's dog walker when she was too busy
to walk Beautybelle herself, once showed her a poem he'd written called
'Grace And The Preacher': something about a girl he was smitten with, and her
religious boyfriend. With Boudreau's permission, Laura snapped up the trifle,
transforming it poetically into 'Grace/and the Preacher/Blown fleets of sweet-
eyed dreams'. Two of the song's later lines must have held special significance
for her, as they were printed on the album's back cover: 'Where is the night
lustre?/Past my trials'. (It's worth noting that in the later, rather perfunctory,
rendition preserved on the *Season of Lights* live album, she omitted all the
cryptic lyrics.)

Laura's quirky eclecticism is given full rein on this track. When she swings
into the line 'Sweet lovin' baby', we could be relaxing into a Brill Building
chorus. But no, harmonic expectations are quickly dashed. Wide-voiced jazz
chords return, always indeterminate, as ambiguous as the lyrics they serve.
To my mind, this is not one of the album's more successful tracks. Sometimes
her improvised starts and stops are just that: mannerisms that leave behind an
impression of unfinished business.

'Captain Saint Lucifer' (Laura Nyro)
Released as a single B-side, August 1970, b/w 'Up On The Roof': US: 92
This track brings together the contradictory features of a composite lover, so
painstakingly explored throughout this album and the one before. The man
she wants to meet will combine a captain's air of authority with the patience
of a saint. Inevitably he'll have a dark side too. When faced with any complex
personality, we only see the light because of the penumbra that surrounds it:
Lucifer (light-bringer in Latin) is also a fallen angel. As in earlier songs, Laura
turns to a mother figure ('a whiz and a scholar too') for advice and support.
One remembers how the singer in 'Stoney End' called out 'Mama cradle me
again', while the character in 'Woman's Blues' was left 'motherless' after her
man deserted her.

According to her friend Barbara Greenstein, Laura wrote the song while
on a vacation to St. Thomas in the Virgin Islands. The island, popular with
American tourists, had been a US possession since its purchase from Denmark,
the previous colonial power, in 1917. Perhaps the Scandinavian connection
set off one of the lyric's many baffling word associations: the reference to 'a
cockleshell on Norway Basin'? On the other hand, as the words tumble over
one another, perhaps it's best not to inquire too closely into meaning. What on
earth is 'a jangle from a congo love chase'? Such lines are sensuous oral poetry,
sound systems that bypass the usual pathways of signification.

This penultimate track on side two may be intended to mirror the second
track on side one, 'Captain For Dark Mornings' – it actually starts with the same
right-hand chords taken at a faster tempo. In a 1994 interview, Paul Zollo asked
her if she had any memories of writing the song. 'Well', she replied, laughing, 'I
guess that was my idea of romance back then'.

When she revived the song for the *Season of Lights* tour in 1976, she allowed
her backing band to jam out for several minutes at the end: it made for a tight
and funky reworking of a Nyro classic.

'New York Tendaberry' (Laura Nyro)
Released as a single B-side, January 1970, b/w 'Save The Country'
'Tendaberry', Laura told the *New York Times* in 1968, was a word she'd made
up to describe the warm, tender core she perceived deep inside the city's
grating exterior. 'I deal in essences', she explained. Whilst she couldn't drive a
car or cook a decent dinner, she had the ability to see 'what is at the centre of
things'. It was a bold move to make this song, with its unfamiliar nonce word,
the title track, but an obvious one: in capturing the city, the song captures the
essence of the whole album. New York is both a place to run away from and
a devotional site she's always drawn back to, because it's more than a city:
'You look like a city/But you feel like a religion to me', she sings at a point of
declamatory climax. Across this album (and its predecessor), there's a sense
of the personal life played out against a cosmic backdrop. God and the Devil
go head-to-head, and the whole drama unfolds not in some celestial realm,

but down here on the streets of her native city. This was her 'very wild time of exploration', as she reflected later.

We know she generally wrote lyrics before music. She certainly did in this case, as she confirmed in an interview with *Downbeat* in 1970. It shows here in the careful sculpting of words. Details abound, in compacted, allusive form – sweet kids in the poor districts, pigeons on the sidewalk, firecrackers, wind and sky, American history from the Pilgrim Fathers to the Founding Fathers. Her synaesthesia is evident too, as the sound of a brush on a snare drum induces a sense of intoxication ('a rush on rum') and the past is folded into colour and music ('a blue note').

Clocking in at just over five and a half minutes, it's the album's longest track. Except for a fleeting brush of chimes in the second verse, it's just Laura and her piano until the very last whispered syllables, where a single note of percussion joins her voice. She uses all her vocal repertoire – cooing over the phrase 'true berry', near-shouting in defiance at 'Now I'm back' – as the melody ranges unpredictably over two octaves.

The sophistication of this love letter to the metropolis has attracted classical and jazz musicians. The most striking cover version is the one by soprano Renée Fleming and cellist Yo-Yo Ma, on Billy Childs' 2014 tribute album *Map to the Treasure*. Childs arranged the song as if there were three central characters – the voice (as storyteller), the cello (as foil, commenting on the story as it's being told), and the piano (a constant underlying presence). Expanding the original to over seven minutes, this ambitious treatment, which rightly scooped a Grammy award, turns the song into full-on music drama. No one can replace Laura – or improve on her – but she continues to inspire others in their own music-making.

2002 Bonus Tracks
'Save The Country' (Single version) (Laura Nyro)
Released as a single A-side, June 1968, b/w 'Timer'
Released as a single A-side, June 1969, b/w 'Eli's Comin''
With The 5th Dimension's version of 'Stoned Soul Picnic' riding high in the charts, Geffen and Clive Davis persuaded Laura that she needed to release a single of her own. The producer would be Bones Howe, who'd also worked on the 5th Dimension record. Recorded at the CBS Studios on Sunset Boulevard, L.A., just a week after the Kennedy assassination, this is a bland, happy-clappy arrangement that lacks the intensity of the album version. It's Laura's music the way someone else heard it. The day after Hubert Humphrey was nominated as presidential candidate at the Democratic Convention in Chicago, a Los Angeles radio station began playing the single once every hour. The broadcast song was preceded by a three-minute tape of the sound of rioting from Michigan Avenue.

The single version was also included on the 1997 retrospective of Laura's work *Stoned Soul Picnic* – not her choice, but part of a compromise reached reluctantly with Columbia Legacy in order to get more of her later material into that package.

'In The Country Way' (Laura Nyro)

Something of a curiosity and a mystery. The only information supplied about this track with the reissue is that it was recorded on 18 May 1971 in Nashville and produced by Richard Chiaro. Chiaro was Laura's booking agent and road manager, not known for his production skills. The date appears to correspond with the recording sessions for *Gonna Take a Miracle*, but those were in Philadelphia, not Nashville. The full-band arrangement here – complete with horn section, harmonica and handclaps – seems, if anything, more in the spirit of the 'Save The Country' single.

When she revived the song at the Bottom Line in 1978, she introduced it by saying, 'I really didn't finish this song'. One understands why: it's negligible. 'This part needs a harmonica', she confides to the audience – perhaps she has her friend John Sebastian in mind as a candidate – as the song peters out in a piano vamp. It's unusual for the perfectionist Nyro to let us in on her thought processes.

Christmas and the Beads of Sweat (1970)

Personnel:
Laura Nyro: piano, vocals, arrangements
Richard Davis: bass
Arif Mardin: conductor, arrangements
Additional musicians on side one:
Barry Beckett: vibraphone
Felix Cavaliere: organ, bells
Roger Hawkins: drums
Eddie Hinton: electric guitar
David Hood: bass
Jack Jennings: percussion
Stuart Scharf: acoustic guitar
Additional musicians on side two:
Alice Coltrane: harp
Dino Danelli: drums
Cornell Dupree, Duane Allman: electric guitar
Joe Farrell: woodwinds
Ashod Garabedian: oud
Ralph MacDonald: percussion
Chuck Rainey: bass
Michael Szittai: cimbalom
Recorded at Columbia Studios, New York City, May 1970
Producers: Arif Mardin, Felix Cavaliere
Engineers: Roy Segal, Tim Geelan
Assistant Engineers: Jerry Lee Smith, Doug Pomeroy
Label: Columbia
Release dates: 25 November 1970 (US), December 1970 (UK)
Chart place: US: 51
Running time: 45:10
Current edition: Sony/Columbia Legacy *Original Album Classics* 2010 CD

For Laura's next album, Geffen suggested Felix Cavaliere as producer. It turned out to be a good fit, even though, by now, Laura's reputation preceded her as someone who was difficult to work with. Cavaliere's group The Rascals had had success as exponents of what the press liked to call 'blue-eyed soul': R&B and soul music made by white artists. He and Laura bonded over shared musical tastes. 'There's a special thing about the New York/Philadelphia/East Coast kind of oldies thing', he told Michele Kort years later. 'You loved that stuff; you grew up on that stuff'. Assured by Laura that The Rascals had been her favourite group at one time, but knowing he had a challenge ahead of him, he brought in Arif Mardin as co-producer and arranger. Mardin – whose previous credits included Dusty Springfield's now-legendary 1968 album *Dusty in Memphis* – was fascinated by Laura's innate musicality, but like many collaborators, struggled to have her pictorial imagery transcribed into the sort of charts that a bass player or guitarist could read from.

Different musicians were assembled for the album's two sides. Side one featured the Muscle Shoals Rhythm Section, named after their base in the northern Alabama town of Muscle Shoals. One of the most prominent American studio house bands of the era, they were masters at creating a southern combination of R&B, soul and country known as the Muscle Shoals sound. It was the sound that characterised Aretha Franklin's 1967 breakthrough, 'I Have Never Loved A Man (The Way I Love You)'. For side two, the producers brought in top-rank professionals, including Rascals drummer Dino Danelli, harpist Alice Coltrane, and guitarist Duane Allman, original leader of the Allman Brothers Band. Interviewed by *Sounds* in 1971, Cavaliere was asked how he'd found working with Laura. He replied:

> She's not very easy to work with, because she's very strict in her ways, her musical ways. She knows exactly what she wants and she's just straight ahead. But outside of the studio, she's a queen; beautiful, beautiful lady.

The session players also found her exacting, but by all accounts, they went out of their way to facilitate her talent; some, like Alice Coltrane, became friends. While Laura's resistance to commercial considerations remained strong, the abrupt tempo changes are less marked than on earlier albums, and with 'Up On The Roof', she accidentally produced the most successful single of her career.

Sessions proceeded slowly, with frequent interruptions for lavish meal breaks. But this time, recording was wrapped up within four months, suggesting a faster work rate than on the protracted *Tendaberry* sessions. As with *Eli*, she derived her album title from the combination of two songs. The phrases 'beads of sweat' and 'Christmas' are like twin coordinates, helping to map a thematic landscape that stretches from urban menace to peace-on-earth. Cavaliere warned her that, with that title, record stores might treat it as a Christmas album and only stock it during the festive season. True to form, she stuck to her guns: that was the title she wanted. For the cover image, she chose a moody pen-and-ink portrait of her, drawn by fan Beth O'Brien. The back cover included lyrics handwritten by Laura (with one or two uncorrected spelling mistakes to add authenticity). The personal touch – handwritten lyrics – would be replicated on another album released that year: Joni Mitchell's *Ladies of the Canyon*.

Overall, *Christmas and the Beads of Sweat* doesn't feel as tightly structured as its predecessors. Perhaps the pressure of writing and recording three albums in as many years was taking its toll. That was certainly Charlie Calello's view when John Stix interviewed him many years later. Calello argued that, while she'd had several years to shape and perfect the songs on *Eli*, as the label demanded more product from her she was forced into recording unfinished material: 'She really wrote songs that were all babies, and she would put them in an incubator and she would nurse them to health. She didn't have the time period to take these songs and nurse them to health'. That's an extreme view of *Tendaberry* and its successor: not one I share.

Christmas and the Beads of Sweat makes a satisfying conclusion to a New York trilogy, and the material is as interesting as anything she'd done previously. But you sense that her focus was shifting. Events from outside were crowding in upon her; the personal had become political. At the same time, she'd made first contact with the alternative belief systems that would become so important for her in later life. Cavaliere introduced her to his spiritual teacher Swami Satchidananda. Laura met the yogi at his ashram, felt an immediate affinity, and for the next few years would practice daily meditation as he had instructed. While in Britain for a concert at the Royal Festival Hall, London, in February 1971, she gave an intriguing interview to Penny Valentine for *Sounds,* which offers some clue to how she positioned the album in her evolving self-understanding. With her first album, she reflects, she'd thought of nothing beyond the songs. Older now, she realises 'There is a world inside and outside each person, and the more together you are inside, the more you can reach out with wisdom'. She talks about how her visits to the Far East had given her a new perspective on her native country. For the first time, she saw America as being 'very dangerous and very sick'. She looks for hope to a group of 'freedom fighters, who are concerned about mankind'. As was common in the counterculture at the time, the line between activism and quietism seems blurred in her thinking. Her primary concern is 'enlightenment'. It's as important to feed starving minds as it is starving bodies, and her music has a role to play in this:

My country is going through a moral revolution at the moment. Not just between colour or men and women, it's all these things and more. It is definitely not evolution we are having, it's revolution ... Most of the time people are unconscious. They can see all those atrocities on television in their own homes daily and stay unconscious to the situation. I do not believe in blowing things up: those buildings will crumble anyway. Consciousness is what I believe in.

Reviews of the album were mixed. *Rolling Stone* – never her greatest fan – complained that her technique had become static and she'd become 'too bloody serious'. Appreciation was growing in Britain, however. Richard Williams in *Melody Maker* declared it 'probably her best album to date', noting that while many of the songs created 'an impression/illusion of greater happiness than before', there was still an underlying 'leitmotif of self-destruction'. *Christmas and the Beads of Sweat* wasn't among the 2002 reissues of her work on CD, apparently because reissue coordinator Al Quaglieri couldn't find an acceptable-quality master: in his words, it had always sounded 'raggedy'. In 2015, a sonically much-improved edition appeared with Sony Japan.

'Brown Earth' (Laura Nyro)

The album opens optimistically. It's a new morning; the singer feels good; there are fresh dreams to deliver. 'God' reappears, but this is not a remote sky god so much as a figure rooted to the spot, 'standing on the brown earth'. She tried to explain this in her 1971 *Sounds* interview: 'I believe in God and that he manifests himself most in people. Yes, I've always had a sense of God, but it's gotten more each year. To me, God is earth, an earthly thing'.

After the trials of the preceding albums, Laura sounds more grounded, more accepting. If love is freely given, then it will be returned, with interest, she seems to be saying. And in a sign that this album will mark the start of a transition to a more outward-facing persona, she links personal fulfilment to broader themes of freedom and fraternity. What saves the lyric from the preachy earnestness that bedevils some of her later work is that she retains a telling eye for detail – the city awakening to 'morning dew', 'ragamuffin boys' and 'watermelon' sellers. But there's no denying the powerful sense of collective spirit in her multitracked vocal, as she sings with gospel fervour, 'Oh what a morning of brotherhood'.

'When I Was A Freeport And You Were The Main Drag' (Laura Nyro)

Released as a single A-side, January 1971, b/w 'Been On A Train'

Like many busy musicians, Laura found that she was only meeting and dating people from inside the business. Dallas Taylor (1948-2015) was one of a number of men she was romantically involved with at this time. Best remembered as the drummer on the debut 1969 Crosby, Stills & Nash album and their follow-up with Neil Young, *Déjà Vu*, Taylor was a troubled figure. One of the first heroin addicts on the Los Angeles rock scene, he would notoriously sabotage Young's guitar solos by changing time signature mid-song. In his autobiography, *Prisoner of Woodstock*, Taylor describes how he found Laura sexy, with her 'exquisitely feminine hands' and 'dark silky hair down to her ass', despite her being 'overweight' and having a 'large nose'. She objected, however, to his escalating drug habit, and this brought the relationship to an end six months after Geffen had first introduced them to each other. Taylor also claims that Laura wrote a song about him – to Geffen's displeasure since as her confidant and manager, Geffen had received no such honour.

Her friends believed this to be the song in question. If so, Laura was the 'freeport' and Taylor the 'drag'. The imagery is amusing, but what does it mean? A 'free port' is one open on equal terms to all shipping, typically one where no customs duties are payable. 'Main drag' is a colloquialism for 'main street'. The sense may be that she was open and accessible to experience, while her smackhead lover was for closing her down, holding her back. He's trying

her patience, 'and that's a lot of patience to lose'. Once again, the personal
and political, private and public life, are entwined. ('The personal is political',
proclaimed the student movement and second-wave feminism of the late-
1960s.) She's mad at her country, and now she's been 'treated bad' by her
lover. She's 'a woman/Waiting for due time', perhaps in expectation of what the
women's movement will promise in the 1970s. (Indeed, when she performed
the song on the *Season of Lights* tour in 1976, she altered the lyric slightly,
replacing 'waiting for due time' with 'and this is my due time', prompting a
round of applause from the audience.)

Musically, this is straighter than many of her earlier tracks. The rhythm section
sets up a solid rock 4/4 rhythm from the outset. The horn section swells the title
line, and over the last iteration of 'drag', she gives an exultant little whoop, as
if she's got something off her chest (or washed that man right out of her hair?).
But nothing with Laura is ever quite straightforward. Although written in her
default key of C major, the song ends unexpectedly on an unrelated D major
chord – an endpoint more satisfactory than the protracted fade-out of 'Brown
Earth' perhaps, but more like a question mark than a full stop.

'Blackpatch' (Laura Nyro)

Whatever setback she described in the previous track, the singer has recovered
her composure here. She's throwing a party. Men can be friends without
being lovers, so there's an invitation on its way to 'Jones'. Again, there's the
concentrated detail that relies on word and sound association, or simply on
puns. The woman on the side street lighting up her lipstick-smeared reefer
and waiting for a 'match' – is it a match from a matchbox, or a man to light her
fire? Perhaps both. She's glimpsed in 'blackpatch': perhaps an islet of light and
shade between buildings. In some rare chat between songs at her Carnegie
Hall concert in November 1969, Laura recalled the clothes hung on clothes
lines strung between apartment blocks where she lived – 'The women hang up
things like little socks and their husbands' muscle shirts' – a vignette that finds
its way into the third verse.

The song is essentially strophic in form; the wilder unconventions of
previous albums are less in evidence now. Her appreciation of gospel piano
patterns is hard to miss. However, mid-track, she diverts to experiment with the
sort of close harmony and call-and-response effect she'll develop with Labelle
on *Gonna Take a Miracle*. 'People, are you ready?', she sings. It's tempting to
hear an echo in this passage of the Curtis Mayfield classic 'People Get Ready' –
a hit for The Impressions in 1965 and surely part of the gospel-influenced R&B
she grew up with. 'People Get Ready' is in a long tradition of Black American
freedom songs that use train imagery, such as 'Wade In The Water', 'The Gospel
Train' and 'Swing Low, Sweet Chariot'. The idea comes from the spiritualist
idea that once one dies, the soul goes on a journey to the afterlife. The next
track will upend that trope to give us, not the train to salvation, but the branch
line to perdition.

'Been On A Train' (Laura Nyro)

Released as a single B-side, January 1971, b/w 'When I Was A Freeport And You Were The Main Drag'.

From the breeziness of 'Blackpatch' to one of Laura's darkest songs and her second reflection on the hazards of drug dependence. No stranger to illicit substances herself, she knew of what she spoke, and her own use sometimes alarmed her contemporaries. Years later, author Barney Hoskyns interviewed Joel Bernstein, photographer to the Laurel Canyon set. Bernstein reflected: 'When Laura Nyro went into a bathroom to do cocaine with her limo driver, I was *horrified*. Because cocaine was *serious shit*'. Fortunately for her and for us, she seems to have been a user, but not an addict.

If the subject of 'Poverty Train' was Laura herself, inspiration for 'Been On A Train' may have come via the death of her 20-year-old cousin Jimmy Nigro from an accidental heroin overdose in October 1969. The lyric is cast in dramatic terms as an intense struggle between the singer and the man she is trying to save. Ultimately, she loses him: he dies 'in the morning sun'. The loss is all the more grievous since the singer has been on this same 'train' herself; it changed her forever, but she managed to get off.

A stunning performance featuring little but voice and piano, this is built out of the simplest elements – slow, gently-syncopated 4ths played in the right hand against alternating 5ths in the bass, creating an open texture of indeterminate passing harmonies. The accompaniment pattern is played over and over with little variation, except for a break into brusque medium-tempo triads as she struggles to save the addict from his fate. Everything depends on the ventriloquial versatility of her voice. After calmly setting the scene, she adopts a sweeter tone, as she holds out the promise of rescue – a 'bright light in the north wind' – to no avail. There ensues a climactic exchange – the addict quietly insists that drugs alone will soothe his pain, and she shrieks, 'No, no/Damn you mister!'. Some listeners – the naysayers who always found Laura 'shrill' and 'hysterical' – would baulk at effects like these. ('I hate Laura Nyro and her blackboard-and-fingernails voice and soulful pretensions', wrote *Rolling Stone*'s Ed Ward in November 1970.) My reply is that she totally inhabits the song, her song: *author*ship confers *author*ity.

Few have dared cover this song since Laura's day. An exception is Rickie Lee Jones, one of the performers who cite Laura as an inspiration. Her version (on *Map to the Treasure*, 2014) pushes the song towards full-on music-theatre mode. Billy Childs' arrangement, including saxophone and string quartet, is ingenious. But in the end, one goes back to Laura's original for its raw power and balance between empathy and anger. In 1971, the original was used as a part-soundtrack to 'Cry' – a solo dance piece created by New York's Alvin Ailey Dance Theater. It remains in the company's repertoire to this day.

'Up On The Roof' (Gerry Goffin, Carole King)
Released as a single A-side, August 1970, b/w 'Captain St. Lucifer': US: 92

Side one closes with a hat-tip to Laura's early enthusiasms. It was the first time she'd recorded a song by anyone other than herself – a harbinger of her next project and of the many cover versions she'd include on later albums.

'Up On The Roof' was first recorded in 1962 by male vocal group The Drifters. Released late that year, the disc became a major hit in early-1963, reaching number 5 on the US singles chart, and the song has found countless interpreters since then. The melody was Carole King's; she'd originally called it 'My Secret Place', putting the emphasis on privacy. Her then-husband and songwriting partner Gerry Goffin preferred 'Up On The Roof', which picked up on the lyric's central image of aspiration. In this song, we're invited to climb the stairs of a tenement block to a place nearest the sky, a safe space for dreaming. It may be a private place, away from the 'hustling crowd', but it's also a potential love nest: a paradise where there's 'room enough for two'.

Laura takes the song at a slower tempo than The Drifters' original. There are several minor word changes, which may simply be the result of negligence (for example, singing 'take' instead of 'face' in the second line of the first verse, which consequently loses the full rhyme with 'space' in line four). More conscious may be her decision to omit the first of the original's three bridge sections: 'On the roof, it's peaceful as can be/And there the world below can't bother me'. Her version is so relaxed, so laid-back, perhaps she felt the lyric didn't need to spell it out. The arrangement is sensitive to the lyric, especially the use of strings with occasional stabbing chords and bowed *tremolo*. The *tremolo* passage is probably the point where, according to Mardin, she asked the violinists to play their part as if it 'shimmered'. After some scratching of heads, they translated this into the musical instruction *sul ponticello*: that is, to bow close to the violin's bridge. Cavaliere remembers this track as an example of her single-mindedness. She did a couple of vocal takes. The producers liked one version; she liked another: 'So, the next day she came in and erased the one we liked, and that was that!', he told *Mojo* magazine in 2022, laughing at the memory.

Here is a classic reimagining of a classic song. One pictures her singing it in her tiny Upper West Side Manhattan penthouse apartment on the 17th floor with its view of the city's back blocks, convinced she had to commit it to vinyl. It would also become a regular in her live sets. In 1970, Carole King recorded a version of 'Up On the Roof' for her own solo recording debut *Writer*, from which it was issued as a single. Comparing this more conventional version with Laura's shows how everything was subsumed by the Nyro style. Rearranged, reharmonised, it somehow became *her* song, even though she didn't write it. The merging of talents – Goffin/King/Nyro – brought Laura a rare kind of success: released as a single, 'Up On The Roof' would be her sole appearance in the Hot 100.

'Upstairs By A Chinese Lamp' (Laura Nyro)

Laura was fascinated by the Far East. She visited Japan on a number of occasions and used Japanese instruments on her later album *Smile*. The inspiration for this song may be nearer to home, however. Her biographer reports that she owned a 'Chinese' lamp, so it's possible that the 'sleepy woman by the window' who dreams of a man who 'takes her sweetness', is Laura herself. We seem to be a long way from New York, though. It's as if the China lamp in her apartment, or the China tea she's drinking, conjure up Orientalist fantasies, visions from the *Arabian Nights*, of merchants and ladies, spring nights and 'scarlet sidestreets'.

'A love poem both objective and compassionate – possibly her most perfect fusion of words and sounds', was critic Ian MacDonald's verdict on this song (*New Musical Express*, 1974), and it's hard to disagree. Try reading aloud a line like 'Winds caress, undress, invite', then listen to this marriage of filigree-fine instrumentation to seductive lyric. An oriental ambience is set from the outset, with piano triads descending pentatonically (the five-note pentatonic scale comprising just five notes, is the basis of much Eastern music). Then Laura's erotically charged vocal begins, supported by guitar and bass with cadenza-like flute flourishes. The arrangement also includes a cimbalom, a Hungarian string instrument not unlike a hammered dulcimer. When the opening chords return, reinforced and louder, it's a moment of tingling excitement. Finally, after Laura is all sung out, comes a delicious instrumental passage. Virtuoso Joe Farrell has switched from flute to oboe, and the cimbalom is joined by an oud: a form of Arabian lute. (Many Western musicians were fascinated by the oud at this time. Nick Drake and Davey Graham were among the British visitors to Morocco in the 1960s who discovered the instrument and sought to imitate its distinct timbre in their guitar technique.)

'Map To The Treasure' (Laura Nyro)

Unusually, we go without a break into this next track. 'Map To The Treasure' inhabits the same sensual universe as 'Upstairs By A Chinese Lamp'. Evidently, Laura saw continuity between the songs, in both theme and style. In this tale of temptation, we're still dreaming of faraway lands, with references to jade, coral and 'perfume from Siam'. But we're also still in New York. When she mentions Spanish Harlem at the very beginning, aren't we circling back to her musical heritage? Back to the Leiber and Stoller production hothouse that gave us the original of 'Up On The Roof'? Let's recall that 'Spanish Harlem' – the 1960 hit for Ben E. King – was his first success away from The Drifters, the group he'd led for several years.

At just over eight minutes, 'Map To The Treasure' is the record's longest track, and is perhaps a little too long for its musical material. The piano starts and ends with slow arpeggiated patterns of 4ths and 5ths between the hands, similar to the effect in 'Been On A Train'. This idea is interrupted mid-song by a manic piano vamp repeated *ad nauseam* at accelerating speed. Since the following lines promise the 'treasure of love', maybe what she intended here was a musical representation of orgasm. If so – pardon the phrase – it's a long time coming. (I find it more convincing on the live recording from the Fillmore East preserved on *Spread Your Wings and Fly*, where the climax is greeted with a burst of audience applause.) Though the dynamic contrasts and tempo changes feel less motivated than in the previous track, that's not to say 'Map To The Treasure' is an underachievement: the vocal is as tender and seductive as any she ever laid down in the studio.

Apart from voice and piano, the ear is caught by delicate harp *glissandi*, courtesy of Alice Coltrane. Laura had become friendly with Alice, widow of John Coltrane and one of the few harpists on the jazz scene, through their mutual interest in meditation and yoga. Alice encouraged Laura to acquire a harp of her own. Laura never made much progress with this difficult instrument, despite taking lessons, but she was drawn to professional players and made inspired use of its sonorities on this and later albums.

'Beads Of Sweat' (Laura Nyro)

After dreams of the exotic in two previous tracks, thoughts are turned firmly back to the city now. New York is mentioned by name, along with the river, railroads and highways. Laura's love of free association produces a compacting of ideas – the rain on the river somehow becomes the rain trickling down a man's neck, which in turn resembles beads of sweat; the singer hears much 'wailing', but it's the wailing of the rain, not of human voices. There's an air of menace, biblical in proportions. Something is coming to devastate the soul, perhaps a great flood. All this *faux* religiosity would be irritating were it not couched in such poetic terms and broadened out into pantheistic world acceptance: the singer looks to God 'although he is the colour of the wind'. Beyond that, the lyric's meaning is opaque. Who are the five boys standing by the river, 'waiting for the virgin snow'? Who is 'Mariah'? (Presumably, with that final letter 'h', not the Virgin Mary.)

After a slow intro, the tempo quickens and we're into a hard rock number – by far the 'rockiest' arrangement on the album – notable for the tight rhythm section and some agile soloing from Duane Allman on lead guitar. Laura again makes generous use of vocal overdubs to create her beloved doo-wop call-and-response effect.

Evidently, she saw this and the final track as part of a whole. In the original handwritten lyrics as they appear on the album cover, the lines beginning 'Come young braves...' are written as if they are part of 'Beads Of Sweat'. They are printed likewise in *Lyrics and Reminiscences* (2004). Yet, in the track division on vinyl, these are clearly the opening lines of 'Christmas In My Soul' – a not insignificant point, because it is in those lines that a form of salvation arrives, written in the 'book of love'. Assuming this album was as carefully structured as the two before it, one wonders if she agonised over the sequencing here. From stormy weather to political protest to the eventual promise of 'joy to the world', we're on an upward gradient of optimism, requiring thoughtful calibration.

'Christmas In My Soul' (Laura Nyro)

A lot of thought went into this lyric. It marks a political turn in Laura's work, and for some, it's the first worrying sign of a didacticism that would come to undermine her artistry. Like her contemporary John Lennon, she makes topical references of a kind that date a song more than anything else can. For Lennon (on his 1972 album *Some Time in New York City*) it was the Attica State prison riots. For Laura, it was the Black Panthers and the Chicago Seven: two *causes célèbres* of the time. In 1969, FBI Director J. Edgar Hoover had declared the Panthers – a Black Power political organisation – to be 'the greatest threat to the internal security of the country'. 1970 was probably the apogee of their support among the American left, the year in which Leonard Bernstein famously hosted a fundraiser party for them with a glitzy celebrity guest list. The 'Chicago Seven' had been charged by the US federal government with conspiracy and other charges related to protests in Chicago during the 1968 Democratic National Convention. Although the conspiracy charges didn't stick, several of the defendants (including Abbie Hoffman and Jerry Rubin) were convicted of crossing state lines with intent to incite a riot. Laura's sympathies also extend here to the 'homeless Indian', the Lenape and Wappinger: the original population of Manhattan Island displaced by European colonists. Her country is dying, she fears, prey to 'The sins of politics/ The politics of sin', and 'Now the time has come to fight'. Yet, for all this outward-facing humanitarianism, the resolution she seeks still appears to be inside herself: 'Christmas in *my* soul'. Revolution in the head before revolution on the streets. The intensity of self that drives her greatest work is still holding, just.

Whatever one makes of the lyrics, there's no denying the measured brilliance of the performance. The discordant bells that ring out the first notes of the carol 'Joy To The World' under the word 'Christmas'; the drum rolls as she addresses a personified 'America'; even the triumphant modulation that heralds the arrival of the title phrase – these touches could tip the song over into melodrama, but her exquisite vocal transcends all that, confounding all objection, evading all pitfalls.

A month after the album was released, she presented the song at the Fillmore East, New York – on this occasion reading the lyric as a poem, in her whispery Bronx accent, without music. The words were slightly altered. 'Madonnas weep' became 'Our mother weeps'. 'Laws in the book of love' was amended to 'Laws of human love'.

Contemporary Track
'Tom Dooley' (Traditional)
Released on *The Nights Before Christmas: New York Broadcast 1970*
'Tom Dooley' is an old ballad which had provided folk royalty The Kingston Trio with a number 1 hit single in 1958. Given Laura's interest in her namesakes,

you wonder if she knew that the song's origins traced back to the 1866 murder of a woman named Laura in North Carolina at the hands of one Tom Dula (pronounced 'Dooley' around those parts, apparently). At the Fillmore East, she has the audience clapping along. It's not her finest moment, and the way she combines it in a medley with the forgettable 'California Shoeshine Boys' using similar accompaniment suggests they draw on the same well of inspiration. Thankfully, it's not a source she returned to with any frequency.

Gonna Take a Miracle (1971)

Personnel:
Laura Nyro: vocals, piano
Nona Hendryx, Patti LaBelle, Sarah Dash: vocals
Norman Harris, Roland Chambers: guitar
Ronnie Baker: bass
Lenny Pakula: organ
Jim Helmer: drums
Vincent Montana Jr.: percussion
Larry Washington: bongos,
Nydia 'Liberty' Mata: congas
Bobby Martin, Lenny Pakula, Thom Bell: string and horn arrangements, using Don
Renaldo's strings and Sam Reed's horns
Recorded at Sigma Sound Studios, Philadelphia, May-June 1971
Producers: Kenny Gamble, Leon Huff
Engineer: Tim Geelan
Mixing engineer: Jack Adams
Label: Columbia
Release date: 17 November 1971 (US), February 1972 (UK)
Chart place: US: 46
Running time: 33:05 (Original LP), 41:49 (2002 reissue)
Current edition: Sony/Columbia Legacy 2002 CD

In late 1970 Laura was touring to support *Christmas and the Beads of Sweat*. There was a new boyfriend in tow, the cherubic Californian Jackson Browne, whose own musical career would prove more enduring than the couple's relationship. After the exertions of completing her great New York trilogy, and possibly blocked in her own songwriting, she turned next to a long-cherished project idea: to record a tribute album, an anthology of the soulful music she'd grown up with. She'd begun adding old favourites like 'Spanish Harlem' and 'He's Sure The Boy I Love' to her setlists. The catalyst for the new disc was meeting three women – Patti LaBelle, Nona Hendryx and Sarah Dash, collectively known as Labelle – whose roots in this music were even deeper than her own.

When they crossed paths with Laura, Labelle were at a transition point in their career. As The Bluebelles, or later Patti LaBelle and the Bluebelles, they'd been a quartet singing what lead singer Patti LaBelle called 'come-back-home-Daddy-please-don't-leave-me love songs'. The defection of original member Cindy Birdsong to The Supremes in 1967 left a trio in search of a new direction. Incoming manager Vicki Wickham took the reins in 1970, advised the change of name to Labelle, and a reinvention of their image and sound. Out went the bouffant wigs and matching dresses; in came afros and jeans. As Patti LaBelle recalls in her autobiography, 'She wanted to change us into a female version of The Rolling Stones'. In the Wickham vision, they were henceforth

59

to be 'three black women, singing about racism, sexism and eroticism'. Their repertoire changed, too: interestingly, the 1971 debut album of the relaunched Labelle included a cover of Laura's 'Time And Love'. Wickham – who'd made her name as a producer on British TV show *Ready Steady Go!* – was also the New York correspondent for UK music paper *Melody Maker*, and it was this connection that coincidentally brought Laura and Labelle together. Wickham had set up an interview with Laura for her paper, and Patti LaBelle tagged along. Laura instantly recognised Patti as one of her teenage heroines, and before the interview was over the two of them were sitting at the piano singing Laura's favourite R&B hits. The rapport was instant. Laura, Patti declared, was 'a black woman in a white girl's body'. It was an obvious step for Laura to invite Labelle to sing backup on her proposed new album.

The choice of songs was largely her own. Laura had decided on producers Kenny Gamble and Leon Huff – architects of the 'Philadelphia sound', that distinct blend of soul with funk and jazz influences that would lay the groundwork for disco later in the decade. To ensure the authentic vibe, recording took place over about a month in the producers' nationally famous Sigma Sound Studios in Philadelphia. Laura insisted on playing piano with the studio house band, which caused some difficulty as they weren't used to her pacing or rhythm. After two weeks, Labelle were still waiting to lay down their vocals. Patti LaBelle – never a fan of the recording process – grew frustrated and bet Huff $1000 that they could complete their vocals in a single day. He took the bet. 'Four hours and 30 minutes and ten songs later, the album was finished, and I had a thousand-dollar bonus', Patti recalled later.

The circumstances of recording explain why the results sound so spontaneous. In revisiting the songs of her youth, Laura recaptures the exhilaration of street performance. A line printed on the album's back cover sums it up: 'Nights in New York, running down steps, into the echoes of the train station to sing'. In a year that saw the release of groundbreaking work in the confessional singer-songwriter genre (the genre she'd pioneered), it might have seemed like a backward step. This was, after all, a long way from Joni Mitchell's *Blue* (released in June of that year.) Laura's piano-playing is noticeably straighter than on previous records, with few of her trademark opaque harmonies. However, the back-and-forth exchanges with her backing singers prompted some of the most heartfelt vocals of her career and testified to the friendship that developed between her and the Labelle women that survived long beyond their time in the studio. 'Laura Nyro *and Labelle*', it says on the cover. In 1971 it was still a little unusual to see a white singer with a black group given equal billing, and while it's Laura's face that fixes the viewer from the front cover, flip the cover over and it's the proud, defiant gazes of Labelle that meet the eye, in a stark monochrome image.

Gonna Take a Miracle attracted some favourable press. 'Though hardcore Nyro freaks might not like it, the record is a delight', declared the *Cincinnati Enquirer*, confident that an album of familiar songs would bring her a new audience. *Rolling Stone* was less enthusiastic, suggesting that 'the Bronx tearjerker' had lost her way in girl-group nostalgia. But the public were on side from the start: good sales figures reflected what was one of her most accessible products.

'I Met Him On A Sunday' (Addie Harris, Beverly Lee, Doris Coley, Shirley Owens)

In retrospect, the girl groups were a fascinating phenomenon. So many flourished in the late-1950s and early-1960s between the decline of early rock 'n' roll and the start of the British invasion spearheaded by The Beatles. Pop historians have estimated there were something like 750 distinct girl groups releasing songs that reached the US and UK music charts between 1960 and 1966.

Formed in 1957 by four teenagers from Passaic, New Jersey, The Shirelles were early out of the blocks. 'I Met Him On A Sunday' was their first release and peaked at number 49 in the US charts in 1958. Later they'd have much bigger successes, for example, in 1960 with the Goffin/King song 'Will You Love Me Tomorrow (the first *Billboard* number-1 by an African-American girl group), but their debut single was notable, not least for being written by the girls themselves. The late-1950s was an era when the roles of songwriter and performer were still rigidly demarcated across much of the industry. In the following decade, artists like Laura would collapse the distinction. In other ways, too, 'I Met Him On A Sunday' might qualify as an early expression of *girl power*. At the risk of overinterpreting a naïve lyric – the man she meets on Sunday, dates on Wednesday and kisses on Thursday, fails to show up on Friday, so by Saturday, it's 'Bye bye, baby'. As romances go, it's fast-moving, but the singer seems to be in control.

The Shirelles later re-recorded the song: their 1966 version was taken faster and had thicker instrumentation. Laura's treatment sticks quite closely to the original single, even down to replicating the handclaps, but strips the arrangement back, initially to voices alone, and slows the tempo even further. What you notice is the energy, as Laura and Labelle trade solo lines and backing harmonies. For all its simple charm, the original sounds wooden, almost mechanical, by comparison.

'The Bells' (Marvin Gaye, Anna Gordy Gaye, Iris Bristol, Elgie Stover)

After a song recalled from childhood, we go without a break to something fresher in Laura's mind. The Originals were the (often uncredited) male backing singers on countless Motown recordings in the late-1960s, including work by Jimmy Ruffin and Stevie Wonder. However, they found their biggest commercial success under the guidance of Marvin Gaye, who co-wrote and produced two veritable hits: the doo-wop influenced ballads 'Baby, I'm for Real' and 'The Bells'. Released as a single for Motown's Soul label in 1970,

61

'The Bells' peaked at number 12 on the *Billboard* Hot 100 and went on to sell more than 1,000,000 copies. Lyrically, it's the simplest proposition imaginable – 'when we kiss, I hear the bells; I hope you hear them too; If you ever leave me, I'll go insane because I'll never hear the bells again'. To this soundtrack, couples slow-danced, lovers smooched, babies were conceived. And, to be fair, The Originals' version – lush and smooth – *was* rather wonderful, although hardly in the musical vanguard of 1970 pop.

Laura sings lead in her arrangement, with soaring descant vocalise from Labelle. She omits some lines and emphasises others. Much more than The Originals' version, this seems to be about desire thwarted rather than reciprocated. 'What do I have to do/To make you feel the tingling too?' she sings with passion. The use of organ to supplement Laura's piano, and the fade-out on the word 'never' set against high strings, are two inspired touches in this classy reimagining of the song.

'Monkey Time' (Curtis Mayfield)

'Monkey Time' – originally '*The* Monkey Time' – was a 1963 hit for Mississippi-born singer Major Lance, peaking at number 8 in the US charts. Not well-remembered now, in the 1960s and 1970s Lance became something of a cult figure in Britain. After touring the UK, where he was supported by Bluesology – the band that included pianist Reginald Dwight, the future Elton John – Lance's older records found success among fans of Northern soul in clubs that played mostly rare and obscure American soul and R&B records. 'The Monkey Time' was one of those infectious up-tempo releases designed to inspire a dance craze. Basically, as the lyrics instruct, you 'twist them hips', 'let your backbone slip', 'move your feet' and 'get on the beat'. It's fun music and nothing more. As football managers are wont to say of their team's performance, it is what it is. Laura's version omits the first verse but otherwise follows Lance's template. It's a simple arrangement, with the rhythm section prominent in the mix.

'Dancing In The Street' (Marvin Gaye, William Stevenson, Ivy Jo Hunter)

Fashioning a medley out of two similar songs, Laura segues straight into the next number. Now the party gets under way in earnest. A familiar hook from the horns announces a much better-known song, 'Dancing in the Street'. Laura would first have heard it in 1964 in the recording by Martha and the Vandellas, whose version reached number 2 on the *Billboard* Hot 100 chart. The idea for dancing came to co-writer William 'Mickey' Stevenson from watching people on the streets of Detroit cool off in the summer in water from opened fire hydrants. The songwriters made sure to include Detroit as one of the cities mentioned in the lyric: 'Can't forget the Motor City'. Whatever the original intent, it's arguable that Martha and the Vandellas took girl-group music to a more serious place. Their songs were released amid the mid-1960s turmoil of race riots and civic unrest. Detroit, for example, erupted in 1967 into riots in which 43 people died. Although lead singer Martha Reeves always insisted this was just a 'party song', many young black demonstrators heard it as a civil rights anthem and a call to action on the streets. The curious are directed at this point to Mark Kurlansky's *Ready for a Brand New Beat: How 'Dancing in the Street' Became an Anthem for a Changing America*: an entire book devoted to pondering whether the original two minutes and 40 seconds of music amount to more than a joyous celebration of dance. Sarah Dash of Labelle is quoted in Kurlansky's book. She contrasts how the song sounded to her in 1964 against how it sounded by 1971:

> I loved 'Dancing In The Street'. It was during the civil rights movement. I thought we will be dancing for freedom, for the right to vote, no more prejudice. It was a time when you could actually see black and white dancing together ... Now, looking back, it had much more meaning than we knew. A new beat, are you ready to re-record it in the '70s? It was about freedom for women. For Laura and three black women, it had a lot of meaning.

Laura's reading combines political awareness with hedonism. The line 'Can't forget the Motor City' becomes *'Don't* forget the Motor City', which it's tempting to interpret as meaning 'Remember Detroit and the 1967 uprising'. Then, trading lines with Labelle, she adds an extended vocal coda that includes some words not in the original lyric. The backing singers offer the somewhat cryptic ad lib, 'I said it looks to me like this could be'. Laura responds with, 'Wish I could shimmy like my sister Kate!' (the title of a completely different song, a jazz standard from the 1920s) followed by a line of her own: 'I'd just dance, dance, dance!'.

One of Motown's signature songs, 'Dancing In The Street' has been recorded by countless other artists. Younger listeners probably came to it through the 1985 duet cover by David Bowie and Mick Jagger: an affably apolitical rendering that reached number 7 in the US charts and was a number-1 single in the UK.

'Desiree' (Lee Cooper, Danny Johnson)
Released as a single B-side, January 1972, b/w 'Gonna Take a Miracle': US: 103
In the mid-1950s, the neighbourhood of 115th Street and Lenox Avenue in Harlem was packed with *a cappella* vocal groups of talented teenagers, each striving to find a sound of their own. Male quintet The Charts came from this background. Essentially one-hit wonders, they released their first single 'Deserie' in May 1957. It reached number 3 on the national R&B charts and was later to feature on many compilations of doo-wop classics. The original version was a slow dance number; a little unusual in having no bridge between the second and third verses, its most striking feature perhaps being Joe Grier's falsetto lead. Grier left the group subsequently, but two of the other founder members – Stephen Brown and Leroy Binns – kept the name going for several

years with new members. The new lineup released an updated version of 'Deserie' in 1967, retitled 'Desiree'. This version was faster, with full band and prominent saxophone, closer in feel to soul than doo-wop.

Though she adopts the later title, Laura's version takes the tempo right down to a point even slower than the 1957 original. The arrangement is stripped back to a minimum: just voice, piano and vibes. Labelle sit this one out as Laura harmonises with herself. In a little under two minutes – the track's duration – there's only time to deliver one of the original three verses, supplemented by repeated invocations of the name 'Desiree'. The effect is intensely erotic, as if Laura wants to remind us that the name in French means 'desired one'. For Laura's growing following among lesbian women, here was an epiphany. As Adele Bertei writes in her 2021 book *Why Labelle Matters*, this was 'the first time I'd hear a woman singing a love song to another woman'. A heterosexual love song had become something else entirely, if the listener so chose. Others would lose themselves in the vocal's mesmeric rapture and not trouble too much over who was addressing whom.

'You've Really Got A Hold On Me' (Smokey Robinson)
And so to a much better-known song, which was a 1962 top-10 hit for The Miracles. The original featured Smokey Robinson on lead vocals and The Miracles' second tenor Bobby Rogers on harmony co-lead, backed by some of the finest Motown session musicians. It's a sinuous ballad in 6/8 time, with a far-from-simple lyric. The sense of being emotionally and physically dependent on another person, yet needing to get away from them, is captured in one internally rhymed line: 'I want to split now, I can't quit now'.

By 1971, the song was already much covered – at John Lennon's instigation, The Beatles had added it to their set as soon as the first import copies of the single arrived in Liverpool, and the fab four breezed through it on their second album *With the Beatles* (1963).

As with 'Desiree', Laura ups the sensuality, although it's not clear this time whether the love object is male or female. After she harmonises with Labelle on the line 'All I need you to do', they swap endearments, Labelle drawing out the word 'hold', and Laura responding with a coquettish cry of 'tighter'. Reverting to a favourite practice in her self-penned songs – tempo variation – she adds a much faster coda with lyrics of her own: 'Hold me baby/I've no time to lose/ Hold me baby and don't turn me loose/'Cause I love you, ooh!'. The repeated 'oohs' that take us into the fade-out suggest we're drawing the curtains on a bedroom scene. *'Laura, you've really got a hold on me'*, might be the typical listener verdict after this sexy performance.

'Spanish Harlem' (Jerry Leiber, Phil Spector)
East Harlem, also known as Spanish Harlem, is an Upper Manhattan neighbourhood with one of the largest Hispanic communities in New York City: mostly made up of Puerto Ricans, with sizeable numbers of Dominican,

Laura Nyro, 1968. A striking image by Bob Cato. (*Columbia/Sony*)

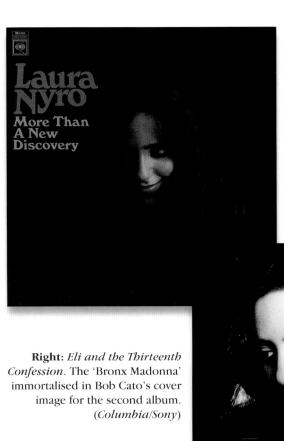

Left: *More than a New Discovery*. Laura's 1967 debut album would prove a source of hit songs for other artists. (*Rev-Ola*)

Right: *Eli and the Thirteenth Confession*. The 'Bronx Madonna' immortalised in Bob Cato's cover image for the second album. (*Columbia/Sony*)

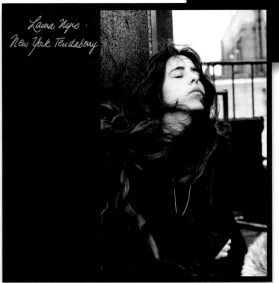

Left: *New York Tendaberry*. David Gahr's cover image captured the urban angst behind Laura's masterly third album. (*Columbia/Sony*)

Right: *Christmas and the Beads of Sweat* was the last instalment of Laura's wide-ranging New York trilogy. (*Columbia/Sony*)

Left: *Gonna Take a Miracle.* Labelle shared cover billing with Laura on this loving hommage to girl groups and doo-wop. (*Columbia/Sony*)

Right: After a long sabbatical, Laura returned in 1976 with the brief but radiant *Smile*. (*Iconoclassic*)

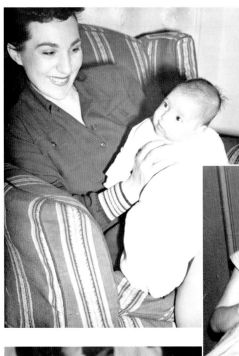

Left: Baby Laura and her mother, Gilda Nigro. (*Jan and Janice Nigro*)

Above: Baby Laura with her mother, Gilda, and father, Louis. (*Jan and Janice Nigro*)

Left: Laura aged about three or four. (*Jan and Janice Nigro*)

Right: Teenage Laura (and friend) at summer camp. Laura was a counsellor and wrote songs for camp events. (*Jan and Janice Nigro*)

Left: Laura around 1973 at home in Danbury, Connecticut. She was always more confident on piano than guitar. (*Janice Nigro*)

Right: Laura, aged about 11, with brother Jan. (*Jan and Janice Nigro*)

Left and below: Laura singing 'Poverty Train' at the Monterey Pop Festival, June 17, 1967. (*D. A. Pennebaker*)

Left: A rare TV appearance, singing 'He's A Runner' on the Kraft Music Hall show, January 15, 1969. (*NBC-TV*)

"I DON'T"

Not every girl gets her man
to say "I do."...but every once in
a while you hear a young girl
who sings and writes songs
with a groovey conviction.

Such an artist is
Laura Nyro.
You'll believe in her
as "We do."

LAURA NYRO
"WEDDING BELL BLUES"

b/w Stoney End KF-5024

Arranged and conducted by Herb Bernstein and Produced by Milton T. Okun, Inc.

VERVE/FOLKWAYS Records are distributed by MGM Records, a division of Metro-Goldwyn-Mayer Inc.

VERVE
FOLKWAYS

Above: Despite press advertising, Laura's 'Wedding Bell Blues' single failed to break into the *Billboard* Hot 100 in late 1966.

Left: Laura was absent from the cover of *Season of Lights*, which instead featured artwork by Rokuro Taniuchi. (*Iconoclassic*)

Right: True to its title, *Nested* revealed a pregnant Laura preparing for motherhood in 1978. (*Iconoclassic*)

Left: Recorded at home in Danbury, Connecticut, *Mother's Spiritual* was a celebration of new birth and new love. (*Line Music*)

Right: *Live at the Bottom Line*: Laura's return to the stage after ten years, with a full band. (*Cypress*)

Left: Nancy LeVine provided a monochrome image of a windswept Laura for *Walk the Dog & Light the Light*. (*Columbia/Sony*)

Right: *Angel in the Dark*: the album Laura was working on at the time of her death. (*Rounder*)

Top: Laura, her brother Jan and son Gil in Ithaca, NY, about 1988. (*Janice Nigro*)

Right: Laura with son Gil, brother Jan and sister-in-law Janice. Ithaca, NY, about 1988. (*Jan and Janice Nigro*)

Right: Laura photographed by Adger Cowans at her cottage in Danbury, Connecticut, in the 1980s. (*Jan and Janice Nigro*)

Left: Laura with her beloved Grandpa Isidore Mirsky in the 1980s. (*Jan and Janice Nigro*)

Right: Laura in 1991 with her partner of later years, Maria Desiderio, Maria's dog Scooty and some of Maria's paintings. (*Janice Nigro*)

Left: In *Musical Architecture*, a 1995 documentary made by her partner, Laura looked back on her musical career. (*Maria Desiderio*)

Left and above: Laura's induction into the Rock & Roll Hall of Fame, 2012. Bette Midler delivered an emotional eulogy. (*Rock & Roll Hall of Fame*)

Left and above: Laura wowed the West Coast in 1970. The *Los Angeles Times* declared her 17 January gig 'an exercise in excellence'.

Left: *The Nights Before Christmas* preserves a radio broadcast from the Fillmore East, albeit in suboptimal sound. (*Unicorn*)

Right: *Spread Your Wings and Fly*, a return visit to the Fillmore East, finds Laura in fine form. (*Columbia/Sony*)

Left: The Carnegie Hall gig was a rare live radio broadcast by a rock artist from this prestigious concert venue. (*All Access*)

RECORDED LIVE AT NEWPORT FOLK FESTIVAL

John Hiatt
Laura Nyro
B.B.King
John Lee Hooker
John Prine
Odetta
Emmylou Harris

Newport

Folk
Festival
1989

Right: Laura's short set at Newport in 1989 was among the highlights on a varied festival bill that year. (*Lexington*)

laura nyro

live from mounta

Left: Another radio broadcast, this one from West Virginia in 1990. (*Blue Plate Music*)

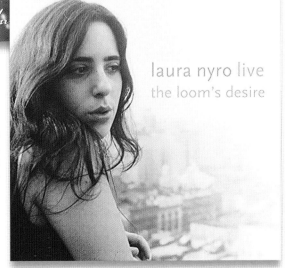

laura nyro live
the loom's desire

Right: Laura's last Christmas shows at the Bottom Line, NYC, in 1993 and 1994, preserved on a double album. (*Rounder*)

Left: Laura's love of Japan – its clothes and customs – is celebrated on the cover of this live recording from 1994. (*Omnivore*)

Right: A poster for the 1994 tour, somewhat incongruously using an image from Laura's Monterey Pop appearance 27 years earlier.

Left: *American Dreamer*, a 2021 boxset reissue of Laura's first seven albums, brought renewed attention to her work. (*Madfish*)

Cuban and Mexican immigrants. In the 1950s and 1960s, large sections of East Harlem were levelled for urban renewal projects, and the neighbourhood was among the hardest-hit areas as the city struggled with deficits, race riots, urban flight, gang warfare, drug abuse, crime and poverty. At the end of the 1950s, Leiber and Spector took the age-old trope of the lover-as-rose and transplanted it into the urban environment, so that now the flower is 'Growing in the street/ Right up through the concrete/But soft and sweet and dreaming' – a reassuring image, reinforced by the distinctive marimba hook that runs through the track (allegedly an uncredited contribution by co-producer Mike Stoller). This song has passed through many hands. It was originally recorded by Ben E. King in 1960. His first hit away from The Drifters – the vocal group he'd led for several years – it peaked at number 10 in the US pop charts. Aretha Franklin released a version in 1971 – the same year as *Gonna Take a Miracle* – that outperformed King's original in chart ranking, but King's would surely have been the earworm that lodged in Laura's teenage brain.

Laura's version is one of the album's bigger arrangements, with the women's combined vocals backed by multiple percussion and a restrained dreamy horn section. She alters the lyric so that it is specifically addressed to a man: the original lyric 'With eyes as black as coal/That look down in my soul' becomes 'With eyes as black as coal/He looks down in my soul'. In the last verse, she's going to 'pick that rose/And watch *him* as *he* grows in my garden'. It's unconventional to represent a man as a rose (or a rose as a man?), but typical of an attitude that marks Laura's thinking as well ahead of the curve. A stand-out track.

'Jimmy Mack' (Brian Holland, Lamont Dozier, Eddie Holland)
Another Motown classic that had been a hit for Martha and the Vandellas in 1967, peaking at number 10 in the *Billboard* Hot 100. They'd actually made the recording in 1964, but Motown shelved it at the time because it was thought to sound too much like a Supremes song. Wiser counsel prevailed by 1967. As a saying of the time went, The Supremes had the style, The Marvelettes had the moves, and The Vandellas had the voices. Though the finished song is clearly about a woman fending off another man's advances and longing for her boyfriend to return, its inspiration may have come from a darker place. The story goes that the idea came to Dozier and Holland after attending a music awards ceremony at which Ronnie Mack's mother accepted an award on behalf of her songwriter son, who'd recently died, aged 23, of Hodgkin's lymphoma.

For my money, this is one of the less inventive reworkings on *Gonna Take a Miracle*. The rhythmic urgency, powered by handclaps, is faithfully carried over from the original; the layered vocals are skilfully done, but somehow the thing doesn't catch fire as other tracks on the album do. Perhaps the song itself isn't interesting enough. Or perhaps it fell casualty to time constraints, reflecting the roughness of a first take. In her liner notes for the 2002 reissue, Amy Linden points to the curious electronic whistling at the start and Laura quietly saying 'Jimmy' as if she's testing the microphone. In Patti LaBelle's words, 'Whenever we made a mistake that sounded cool, we left it in'. But I recognise that for others, the song has a significance since lost to history or isolated in personal experience. In 1967, and still in 1971, how the chorus must've resonated with an American public divided by the Vietnam War. 'Jimmy Mack, when are you comin' back?'. Families desperately wanted their boys to come home, and even an upbeat little love song could be pressed into service to carry that emotional burden.

'The Wind' (Nolan Strong, Juan Guitierrez, Willie Hunter, Quentin Eubanks, Bob Edwards)

Speaking to Michael Snyder of the *San Francisco Chronicle* towards the end of her life, Laura recalled that the first rock 'n' roll song she ever heard was 'The Wind'. It struck her as 'earthy romantic music that inspired more leaps of faith and less cynicism'. That would've been the original 1954 version by Detroit-based vocal group Nolan Strong and the Diablos. Later, as Laura began singing doo-wop with friends in subway stations, she took the song into her repertoire. By now, there was another recording out there, by local New York group The Jesters, whose 1960 single of 'The Wind' peaked just outside the *Billboard* Hot 100. But you can see why the 1954 original would stick in the mind. With Nolan Strong's high tenor voice (an influence on the young Smokey Robinson) and the production's overly heavy reverb, The Diablos' version captures more of the street spirit of doo-wop. While more commercially successful, The Jesters' version is smoother.

After a short intro on vibes, Laura creates her version alone, as she had done on 'Desiree'. With some churchy reverb effects, she builds up multitracked backing vocals to suggest the soughing of the wind while her solo soars aloft. She omits the cringe-inducing spoken-word lyric of the original, leaving just the song's central proposition: that though the lover may be gone, 'Love lingers on/In a dream that the wind brings to me'. There are a few minor changes to the remaining lyric: principally, amending the pronouns so that the song is now addressed to a man. As if to show how she's absorbed the number into her own idiom, she ends on an ambiguous piano chord that wouldn't have sounded out of place on *New York Tendaberry*.

'Nowhere To Run' (Brian Holland, Lamont Dozier, Eddie Holland)

A total shift of gear, and the album's third genuflection to Martha and the Vandellas. On the 1965 original, producers Dozier and Holland and the Funk Brothers band gave the song a broad, energetic instrumental sound similar to their earlier treatment of 'Dancing In The Street', even using snow chains as percussion alongside tambourine and drums. Like 'You've Really Got A Hold On Me', it's a song about co-dependence in a relationship: 'I know you're no good for me, but you've become a part of me' must count as a key line.

Laura's update matches the energy levels of the original. No snow chains detectable, but there is nimble-fingered bass-playing from Ronnie Baker, and dramatic close harmonies from Labelle on lines like 'Everywhere I go, your face I see' (one of a number of clumsy phrasal inversions in the lyric that would never work on the page). As on several other tracks, she adds an extended full-on gospel finale, some of it *a cappella* with the girls, repeating *ad nauseam* the lines 'No, no, ain't got nowhere to run to/Ain't got nowhere to hide'. Many gospel songs feature so-called *drive* sections like this, where the background singers repeat a single line over and over, while the lead singer ad-libs. It makes 'Nowhere To Run' the album's longest track, at just over five minutes. To my mind, it feels like a failure of invention when the flame of reinvention has burned so brightly up to this point. Adele Bertei – keen to read lesbian subtexts into every stage of the singer's career – interprets this passage as Laura 'hiding' her true love inside a 'white hetero mask'. For academic Mark Anthony Neal, the repetitive chanting shows how women have 'nowhere to hide' within 'highly structured patriarchal and masculine spaces'. Less provocatively, Michele Kort suggests in her biography that Laura's aim was to arouse a 'revivalistic spirit'. Perhaps – like a revivalist meeting – to get it, you really have to *be* there, in the moment.

'It's Gonna Take A Miracle' (Teddy Randazzo, Bobby Weinstein, Lou Stallman)

Released as a single A-side, January 1972, b/w 'Desiree': US: 103

This song was originally intended and written for all-male New York vocal group Little Anthony and the Imperials, but they never recorded it due to a royalty dispute with the song's owners. Instead, the honour went in 1965 to The Royalettes, a short-lived four-girl group from Baltimore. 'It's Gonna Take A Miracle' would be The Royalettes' greatest success, peaking just outside the top 40 on the *Billboard* Hot 100. Their original of the song – freighted with heavy strings – was a grandiose production, typical of the MGM label. Deniece Williams was to find greater chart success with her cover in the early-1980s, but The Royalettes' lead vocalist Sheila Ross takes some beating. In that spirit, Laura's version comes across as respectful, wisely disinclined to take chances. Her arrangement – one of the record's bigger treatments – is more discreet in its use of strings than the original, but it swells out magnificently in the middle eight to create contrasts of tone and dynamic more subtle than anything The Royalettes could muster. It's an exultant finale and a classy endpiece to an album of classics.

This was one of two Nyro cuts from the album ('Desiree' was the other) used in the soundtrack to the 2004 film *A Home at the End of the World*. In the movie – based on a novel by Michael Cunningham – rebellious teenager Bobby Morrow befriends gawky Jonathan Glover in high school and becomes a regular visitor to the Glover home, where he introduces Jonathan and his mother Alice (played by Sissy Spacek) to marijuana and to the music of Laura

Nyro. 'She's my goddess', Bobby tells Alice as they slow-dance, in a pot-fuelled haze, to this track.

Bonus Tracks
'Ain't Nothing Like The Real Thing' (Nickolas Ashford, Valerie Simpson)

The 2002 reissue included four live tracks taken from Laura's solo concert at the Fillmore East, New York City, on 30 May 1971. (The whole gig was released in 2004 under the title *Spread Your Wings and Fly*.) 'Ain't Nothing Like The Real Thing' was a 1968 Marvin Gaye & Tammy Terrell hit that Laura had planned to record for *Gonna Take a Miracle*. However, like several other shortlisted songs, it didn't make the cut. The live version here is perfunctory, lasting little under a minute. She vamps for a while on piano, as if undecided what she's going to perform next, sings the title line several times, then segues into…

'(You Make Me Feel like) A Natural Woman' (Gerry Goffin, Carole King, Jerry Wexler)

Laura would, of course, have known this song from Aretha Franklin's 1967 single. An intriguing question is how familiar she'd have also been with Carole King's recording, which appeared in February 1971 on King's multi-platinum-selling LP *Tapestry* – a version for voice and piano that was some way removed from the orchestrated 1967 arrangement and was a template for performing the song solo. Laura grasps the nettle and delivers a thrilling performance, pounding out the piano chords before climbing to the top of her register for the ecstatic line, 'Oh, baby, what you've done to me'.

'O-o-h Child' (Stan Vincent)

In concert, Laura liked to create medleys by combining her own songs with cover versions. At a London concert recorded for BBC Television in May 1971 (since wiped, to the broadcaster's eternal shame), she sang 'Timer' (from *Eli*), then went into this number: a minor gem of Chicago soul which had been a hit for family group The Five Stairsteps in summer 1970. Back on home soil a few days later, she repeated the medley at the Fillmore East. She rewords several lines slightly from the original but leaves the song's simple message of optimism intact: 'Things are gonna get easier' and 'Things'll be brighter'. At this point, motherhood was still in the future for Laura. Some years down the track – in songs of her own like 'To A Child' – she'd recapture the simple tone of consolation she expresses here.

'Up On The Roof' (Gerry Goffin, Carole King)

With a sigh of 'anyway', she eases into the last number of the medley. The balance isn't ideal on this live recording, the piano too prominent against the voice. Compared to the considered effects of the studio version on *Christmas and the Beads of Sweat*, this sounds a bit raw. But what the performance lacks in polish, it makes up for in honesty, and the audience applause is well deserved.

Contemporary Tracks
'American Dove' (Laura Nyro)
Released on *Spread Your Wings and Fly: Live at the Fillmore East, May 30, 1971* (2004)

'American Dove' was one of two new songs introduced on tour in 1970 and 1971 that never reached the studio. This is a shame, since it's a powerful call for peace, intoned over plaintive chords with subtle modulations from F to G to B flat. Slower and less strident than 'Save The Country', it draws on the same gospel imagery. The dove of peace makes a reappearance. 'I'll never sell my soul', Laura assures us, confident that 'The young lord's come/To bring liberty to everyone'. It's 1971, so the Vietnam conflict is never far from anyone's thoughts: the song tells of a boy who 'ain't come home from war/ Don't they honour life no more?'. But hope springs eternal, as surely as the sun rises every morning: 'It's been a long time comin', I mean love/Spread your wings and fly, American dove'.

With an attentive ear for classic Americana, British-Pakistani songstress Rumer stumbled across 'American Dove' and took to performing it in concert in 2012, bringing renewed attention to this neglected song.

'Mother Earth' (Laura Nyro)
Released on *Spread Your Wings and Fly: Live at the Fillmore East, May 30, 1971* (2004)

Another song known only from this recording, 'Mother Earth' is a prototype for all those eco-anthems to come later in Laura's career. It was on the setlist for her BBC TV concert in May 1971, of which no recording survives, but thankfully we have this live performance from later the same month. The Fillmore East audience have grown boisterous, and she circles round and round the opening chords as if to induce an appropriate calm for what follows. It starts out as a love song ('I love him, body and soul'), before taking a prophetic turn. In her later work, there will be no swooning over men: heroines supplant heroes. Now, she moves into a panegyric addressed to the Earth. We have to *believe* in Mother Earth as if with religious fervour, she implies, because the Earth is touched by divine love. We owe our Earth-mother respect since the 'first step to heaven/Is to pay your dues'. However far we roam – even to the snowy wastes of the Arctic where mariners lost their lives in search of the Northwest Passage – we're returned to the 'heart'. The Earth *hears* us. It's a pleasingly noncommittal sketching of ideas which she'd later drive home with less subtlety. Yes, compared to her other songs of the time, it's musically unadventurous, but she gives a mesmerising, hypnotic vocal, much of it precariously high in her register. As soft repeated chords fade away, you wonder why she never worked this one up in the studio.

'Ain't No Mountain High Enough' (Nickolas Ashford, Valerie Simpson)

Released on *Laura Nyro: The Broadcast Archives* (2020)

This rarity was recorded at Kosei Nenkin Kaikan concert hall in Tokyo during Laura's Japanese tour in November 1972. The CD box set on which it appears is what's politely called a 'grey-area release' – material that has already appeared on YouTube, in this case, uploaded by a Nyro superfan and then marketed by less-conscientious souls. I include it here, despite the somewhat murky sound quality, because it's the only known recording of Laura covering this Motown classic. Her resort to spoken-word in the verses suggests that she was following the reworking of the song from Diana Ross' 1970 solo version rather than the Marvin Gaye/Tammi Terrell original. She adds her customary vocal embellishments, without merely dancing around the note. It's not easy in a solo performance to simulate a call-and-response effect on the lines 'No wind (no wind), no rain (no rain)', but she gives it her best shot.

Smile (1976)

Personnel:
Laura Nyro: vocals, piano, guitar, wood block
John Tropea, Hugh McCracken, Joe Beck, Jeff Mironov, Jerry Friedman, Greg Bennett: guitar
Will Lee, Richard Davis, Bob Babbitt: bass
Chris Parker, Allan Schwartzberg, Rick Marotta: drums
Jimmy Maelen: tambourine, wood block
Nydia 'Liberty' Mata, Carter C.C. Collins: congas
Rubens Bassini: shaker
David Friedman: vibraphone
Michael Brecker, George Young: flute, saxophone
Joe Farrell: saxophone
Randy Brecker: trumpet
Paul Messing: triangle
Nisako Yoshida, Reiko Kamota: koto
Recorded at Columbia 30th Street Studio, New York City, autumn 1975
Producers: Charlie Calello, Laura Nyro
Engineers: Don Puluse, Tim Geelan
Assistant Engineers: Jay Messina, Lou Waxman, Stan Tonkel
Label: Columbia
Release dates: February 1976 (US), March 1976 (UK)
Chart place: US: 60
Running time: 31:57 (Original LP), 40:55 (2013 reissue)
Current edition: Iconoclassics 2013 CD

By 1971, Laura had accomplished a prodigious amount. She'd released five albums in five years and composed several dozen songs in which she'd laid bare her emotional life with a candour rarely seen in popular music. It was time to move on. In 1971, she met and fell in love with carpenter David Bianchini. As a decorated Vietnam veteran, he wasn't an obvious match for her anti-war sensibilities, but friends recalled how she responded to Bianchini's virile, romantic image; indeed, she seems to have made much of the running in their courtship, and talked him into marriage in November 1971. They moved into a house in Bianchini's hometown Gloucester, Massachusetts (although Laura retained her Manhattan apartment).

It felt as if a second phase of her career had begun. Her original contract with Columbia had expired with *Christmas and the Beads of Sweat*. The terms of her new contract – finalised on the eve of her marriage – seem quite extraordinary in retrospect. Assuming a productivity level to match her early peak, the contract required an album a year for the next five years. You sense that the pressure was proving to be too much. After playing some dates in Japan in 1972, she announced she was taking a break from recording and performing. The break would stretch into a four-year absence from the public arena. During this time, she moved again – to the simple cottage among woods in Danbury, Connecticut, that she would call home for the rest of her life. Quite a turnaround for the woman who'd told *Newsweek*'s Hubert Saal in 1969:

The city penetrates everything I do. I'm aware of how tough the city is, but I thrive on that. Sometimes I have to get away, but I could never leave it. I see too much beauty here. I'm intense. Sometimes it's hard for me to slow down. The city is a match for me.

Some feared she'd retired from the industry. Not so. She continued to work on her songs – while admitting she was less prolific than of old – and by 1975 had enough material (well, almost) for a new album. In need of a dependable producer, she turned back to old friend Charlie Calello. She wanted a jazz feel to the album. (Jazz crossover was in the air – In 1975, Joni Mitchell had released *The Hissing of Summer Lawns*, her most jazz-inflected album to date.) Accordingly, Calello hired a number of esteemed jazzmen for sessions back in the city: including the versatile Brecker Brothers – Randy and Michael – on trumpet and saxophone, respectively. Like Laura's other arrangers, Calello grappled with her quirky musical instructions. Preparing one guitar-led track for *Smile*, he asked what she wanted the song to sound like. 'Charlie, I want it to be like my chair', she replied, pointing to a piece of plain wooden furniture. He interpreted this as meaning acoustic, organic in nature, with no brass: 'Delicate and cared for and curved in the right places'. Happily, when they reached the studio, Laura confirmed that the results sounded like her chair. However, the artist/producer relationship wasn't always as harmonious as their previous collaboration on *Eli*. Calello felt that Laura was no longer willing to take his advice, and he was unimpressed with some of the new material. As he later told John Stix: 'Each writer has a window of opportunity that is available to them when they are prolific and really writing their style ... she didn't have that window anymore'.

The album is short at just under 32 minutes, and listeners may feel shortchanged. The predominant mood is mellow, which was perhaps a true expression of the stasis she'd now reached – or, as she put it to interviewer Michael Watts: 'The rhythm of me, of my body, is more gentle than the crash-bang trip of the music business'. The divine and diabolic cosmic forces that promised or threatened in earlier albums are in retreat. The devil has taken the hint – and taken the hindmost. No longer is she a woman being pursued. Which is not to say the album isn't freighted with emotion. Laura suffered personal loss during the recording sessions: Gilda Nigro died in August 1975 of ovarian cancer – the same cruel disease that would take her daughter's life 21 years later – and the album is dedicated to her.

The cover art featured Laura's handwritten lyrics, adorned with doodles of curlicues and blossoms, and casual photos of the singer taken in Japan by new friend Patty DiLauria. Reviewers were divided as to whether this fresh Laura compared favourably to the old one. *Rolling Stone*'s Dave Marsh suggested she should 'Knock it off and go back to being the crazy kid from the Bronx we all used to love'. Reception in Britain was a little better. Penny Valentine (*Street Life*) saluted the new release as 'a breakthrough for optimism'. For Charles Shaar Murray in *New Musical Express*, the only albums of 1976 that came within 'breathing distance' of *Smile* were Dylan's *Desire* and Bowie's *Station to Station*.

Personally, I see it as a rather uncertain reaching out for a new direction. The first five albums constitute a satisfying unity – a masterly trilogy, bookended on one side by an LP of her versions of her songs that would be made famous by others, on the other by a disc of her versions of other people's songs. The five studio albums she made in the remainder of her life contain fine work, but the pressure is off and the temperature drops.

'Sexy Mama' (Al Goodman, Sylvia Robinson, Harry Ray)

As the only cover version on *Smile*, this opening track provides continuity with Laura's last project and is also a pointer to where she was headed. In her comparative anonymity in Danbury, she stayed in touch with the music business by playing albums and listening to the radio. 'Sexy Mama' was a song she first heard on the radio. A minor hit in 1973 for male vocal trio The Moments, the original was a proto-disco exercise in seduction technique: hot and breathy and none-too-subtle. The singer promises to 'open them love gates', after which 'There's gonna be a love explosion'. It's the erotic territory that Laura had crossed with a far more sophisticated lyric in 'The Confession'.

Laura's version of 'Sexy Mama' is lazy and languorous. You feel she's drawn more to the second word of the title than the first, making this an appropriate *entrée* to an album dedicated to her late mother. She begins by speaking a single word – 'strange' – as if she's inviting us into her distinctive sound world, before strumming a guitar intro. (Her guitar-playing was never more than functional; the piano was her instrument.) The voice is warm, riper than on earlier recordings. She picks and chooses from the original lyric, repeating the lines that appeal to her, while Joe Farrell's relaxed saxophone snakes in and out of the arrangement. The track sets a sanguine tone for what's to follow.

'Children Of The Junks' (Laura Nyro)

The rest of the songs are all Nyro originals and amount to an autobiography of her years away from the business. This song, written some years before on a trip to Hong Kong, reflects her long-term fascination with the Far East. She has left the imagined armchair Orient of 'Upstairs By A Chinese Lamp', to go on location among the junks and Chinese dragon boats. As before, *chinoiserie* is evoked by pentatonic touches in the piano part, but overall it's a much less inventive track than 'Upstairs By A Chinese Lamp', failing to match its poetic detail and capacity to surprise, despite Richard Davis' agile bass part and some rather endearing multitracked cooing of the city name 'Kowloon'.

'Money' (Laura Nyro)

Now it gets more interesting, as Laura seems to recover some of the fury in her soul. In 1994 she told interviewer Paul Zollo that 'Money' is about 'all the hassles of the ego world converging'. Her relationship with manager and friend David Geffen was never straightforward, and during her spell out of the public eye, it had deteriorated beyond repair. In the late-1960s, each needed the other. Geffen launched his own career as a music mogul on the back of hers as singer-songwriter – for someone as unworldly as Laura could be, the young impresario offered the commercial acumen needed to bring her talent to the marketplace. Geffen owned half of her publishing company Tuna Fish Music, which by the late-1960s was already earning $200,000 a year for her. Viewing her back catalogue as her best asset, Columbia wanted to buy it. There was much to-ing and fro-ing over the market valuation. As bitterness grew between Geffen and Columbia President Clive Davis, Laura was caught in the middle. Simultaneously, her recording contract was up for renewal. Geffen had formed his own label, Asylum Records, and assumed that Laura would sign with him. Ever the showman, he even tipped off the press that it was a done deal, which was untrue. She preferred to re-sign with Columbia – the home of Bob Dylan and Barbra Streisand and a label that had given Laura extraordinary creative freedom in the past. When she conducted negotiations directly with Davis, Geffen felt betrayed. The partnership was broken; Geffen and Laura spoke only a few times after their falling-out.

Her bitterness over the Geffen affair finds its way into 'Money'. 'I feel like a pawn in my own world', she sings. Whereas 'A good friend is a rare find', she's learned that 'A good pimp's gonna rob you blind'. Her disillusionment with the music business is captured in one simple line: 'I found the system and I lost the pearl'. But the critique extends further than her own industry. She told John Rockwell of *Rolling Stone* that, in this song, she heard 'cylinder rhythms: the turning of the city, the turning of business'. And indeed, in a later verse, she turns her fire on industrial fishing (perhaps thinking of her beloved tuna?) – a first flash of the eco-welfare concerns that will become so important for her later. The music has an appropriately *driven* feel, dominated by Michael Brecker's saxophone and the tight rhythm section of Bob Babbitt and Allan Schwartzberg. The choruses are gutsy and melodically strong. But the play-out on wordless multitracked vocals is much too long and threatens to dampen the flame she's lit with some of the album's most incisive lyrics.

'I Am The Blues' (Laura Nyro)

In this, the first of the album's two songs referencing the colour blue, what once was a malignant force, now appears tamed. Where the blues might once have engulfed her, she is now in control, embodying the threat in order to neutralise it, rather as a shaman might wear the pelt of a dangerous animal: '*I* Am the blues'. The lyric seems to describe an upward movement as if she's rising above melancholy or despair. Along the way, she observes the familiar red taillights of urban traffic and looks down at her own 'love for sale shoes'. (Perhaps a joke on herself. She was known to wear some pretty tacky outfits.)

Calello's arrangement brilliantly captures the progress from earthbound to skybound. At the start, it's all swirling vibes and piano as Laura is alone with her 'smoke and ashes'. Later, as she imagines flying through the sky 'like superfly' – the blues vanquished – a brass section kicks in, foregrounding Randy Brecker's muted solo trumpet. This leads to an artfully balanced dialogue between voice and trumpet. Here, the longish jazz outro is well-judged, justified, lovable, and expressive of the altitude she's reached: 'Flying so high/A plane in the sky'.

This song actually dates from the era of the trilogy. She performed an earlier version at the Fillmore East in 1971 (preserved on *Spread Your Wings and Fly*), which has much the same melody but many differences of lyric. In 1971 she leans much more insistently on the title line. The sense of identification with the blues is stronger than the sense of transcendence, with the result that the song in its earlier incarnation feels more visceral but less compassionate. As Penny Valentine suggested in her 1976 review of *Smile*, Laura 'misses the blues because she needs them as an emotional resource for her work, but they are no longer an integral part of her existence'.

'Stormy Love' (Laura Nyro)

Laura's marriage had started to unravel after a couple of years. Who knows what goes on inside a marriage, but the evidence collected by biographer Michele Kort suggests a familiar pattern. A man married to a wealthy and successful woman, supposedly her protector – her 'captain' in Laura's terminology – is unsure of his own role, unsure of who he *is* other than being her husband. They argue, separate, come back together, drift apart. Bianchini apparently suffered post-traumatic stress from his experiences in Vietnam and attributed many of their marital difficulties to his state of mind. The song reflects on a failed relationship. A partner who was everything to her, who could make everything come right, who could make her sing, is now seen in the rearview mirror. She's resolved to start again, with no more tears, welcoming a chance to spread her wings. Yet she's changed – as all feeling people *are* by intimate relationships: 'And I'm gonna love again/Though I'm never gonna be the same'. The mood is one of spent emotion co-opted into an action plan. Personal experience is invoked, then translated into a general truth, as the lyric moves from 'Baby, it's a stormy love' to the later proposition, 'Baby, it's a stormy world'.

The setting on this side two opener is relaxed, with no piano (Laura possibly on guitar – it's not clear from the liner notes), and Nydia Mata's congas high in the mix. I find the whole effect somewhat lethargic, but others will hear a sincere depiction of the calm after the storm.

'The Cat-Song' (Laura Nyro)

A change of gear brings us to a lively comedy song. Perhaps nothing illustrates the transition from the intensity of the New York trilogy to the gentler, more transparent tone of the Danbury years than to compare Laura's two cat songs. In the city, she had a cat called Timer, but her song of that name seems to be about a whole lot more than furry felines. This song poses no such challenges to the interpreter. She identifies with her cat Eddie, taking on his voice, and envying his uncomplicated life given over to eating and sleeping. When he's up and about, he has that mysterious air of purpose unique to his breed. Asked where he's going, he replies, 'On my merry way'. While human beings squander their lives' capital ('You wheel and you war'), Eddie is content simply to *be* in the now.

This is one of her most charming conceits, sung to the accompaniment of jaunty syncopated piano chords. In two and a half minutes, it's all over, and we've learned all we need to know about Eddie and his worldview. With its girl-group-style backing vocals, the song also recalls the treatments on *Gonna Take a Miracle* and something of that album's *joie de vivre*.

'Midnite Blue' (Laura Nyro)

As her marriage broke up, Laura found companionship in new love Gregory Royce Bennett. Usually reticent about discussing her private life, she was happy to introduce him to visiting British journalist Michael Watts in early 1976. Watts noted:

> She seems very happy with Bennett. They sing and play guitar together, and silences linger between them. He's from Ohio; a quiet, lithe man, who might be a Vietnam vet with his ponytailed hair, his khaki jacket and desert boots. He plays so well, that John Hammond (noted producer), who came to dinner some time ago and heard him, wants him to record.

Elsewhere in the interview, Laura referred to Bennett as her 'gypsy man', and he was surely the inspiration for this untroubled love song. Indeed, as 'Greg Bennett', he's one of two guitarists credited on the track. Laura's lyric describes someone who makes her laugh, someone 'shy, sly, gypsy high'. Her synaesthesia must play a part too – 'Midnite Blue' is the distinctive dark shade of blue named for its resemblance to the apparently blue colour of a moonlit night sky around the full moon. When she sings 'I need his melody/Oh midnite blue/Come to me', she's hearing blueness in his music; perhaps she even reads his personality as dark blue. If music equates to colour for a vivid imagination such as hers, maybe chromatic variety corresponds to the variety of human types.

Returning obsessively to the same leisurely two-chord sequence, the song doesn't *go* anywhere. It doesn't *want* to go anywhere. The most charitable interpretation is to view it as a plateau of contentment – and we all need those sometimes.

'Smile' (Laura Nyro)

'Midnite Blue' included the line 'Smile all you want'. Smiling is the album's theme, and it carries us over to the title song. The buoyant mood continues in this concluding track. The world may have gone mad, Laura sings, 'but our love is a peace vibe'. Although a 'non-believer', she believes in her lover's smile. Sensory impressions of landscapes and cityscapes merge in upbeat lyrics, punctuated by George Young's jazz-like saxophone breaks, and concluding (like Molly Bloom's soliloquy in Joyce's *Ulysses*) with the single word of acceptance: 'Yes'.

At one point, we seem to be back in New York, as she refers to 'the kiss of the cunt-tree night'. Innocent listeners will hear this line as 'country night', but no, the pun is spelt out in the printed lyrics. Of course, someone as cultured as Laura would've known Hamlet's bawdy exchange with Ophelia in Shakespeare's play, where the prince teases the lovelorn girl about 'country matters'. Nearer to home, though, 'cunt tree' is (I'm reliably informed) a slang term for the Bradford pear – a type of deciduous tree that in the 1960s was planted throughout New York and widely along the US eastern seaboard, where its white, raunchy-smelling flowers perfume the air in spring.

Given that the Bradford pear is an American cultivar of a species native to China and Vietnam, there may be all manner of cultural exchange going on here. The strongest driver of this track is Laura's love of the Orient. Lyric references to strangers, mountains and snow suggest remote climes – perhaps somewhere like the distant view of the snowcapped Mount Fuji, so dear to the artist Hokusai. Laura told Charlie Calello that she wanted a Japanese sound. And so, with a little help from the Japanese embassy, a pair of koto players were recruited. (The koto is a plucked half-tube instrument rather like a zither. The most common type has 13 strings, with movable bridges to allow tuning.) It's their distinctive sound that kicks off the song. They return later, as the track ends in a free-form jam between East and West: echo-laden flute and stand-up bass trading licks with the koto players. Apparently, Laura mapped out the parts herself. It's notoriously difficult to integrate Oriental instruments with those using Western pitch, but the results here are rather lovely. Under the separate title 'Mars', this instrumental would be recreated with Western musicians alone on her 1977 tour.

Bonus Tracks
'Someone Loves You' (Laura Nyro)

Three demos were added to the 2008 Japanese reissue of the album and its later US release on Iconoclassic. Probably dating from 1974, they all sound like works-in-progress, or sketches for songs that she then revised into other shapes. 'Someone Loves You' uses the syncopated piano figure from 'The Cat-Song' but ties it to a simple love lyric. Humans not kitties. The 'red light' that's going to 'shine on his kisses', anticipates a promise in 'Stormy Love': 'I'll turn my red light on/Let it shine when the sun is gone'. She finishes, almost apologetically, with a cough. This really is a glimpse into the workshop of her making.

'Get Me My Cap' (Laura Nyro)

This one opens with the oriental chords of 'Upstairs By A Chinese Lamp' (in altered rhythm) and seems to reflect a similar milieu. During Laura's marriage to Bianchini, the couple lived for a month on a houseboat on Lake Dal in Kashmir. At the time, Laura envisaged calling her next LP *Red Lantern*. Thinking ahead to a possible album cover, she asked her husband to photograph a Kashmiri man in a boat holding a red lantern – which may explain the phrase she uses here: 'Shining like a red lantern'. The line 'Throw away the death that you've seen' could refer to Bianchini's struggle to put his Vietnam experiences behind him. References to 'captain' and feeling like a 'tramp on a steamer' recall a harebrained scheme of Laura's to buy a tugboat and install her symbolic 'captain' as a real captain: a plan that came to nothing when she found she had no sea legs. The recycling of the line 'I feel like I'm way in a deep dream' in the later song 'Smile', suggests that she'd moved on from whatever prompted this abandoned draft. Still, it's an intriguing vignette, enlivened by handclaps and her own overdubbed harmonies, that deserved fuller development.

'Coffee Morning' (Laura Nyro)

A song revisiting her earlier style. The gentle undulating chords of the opening take us right back to 'Buy And Sell' from the first album, while the apparent structural freedom is in the line of descent from *New York Tendaberry*. Again, this voice-and-piano sketch may date from the time of her marriage, judging by the line 'I'll forget the war and the pain in my head'. You're carried along on the rhapsodic rise-and-fall of Laura's voice, even if many of the words are hard to discern. In the liner notes to the 2013 reissue, Michele Kort hears the lyrics as 'almost a stream-of-consciousness plea to her lover', and I wouldn't disagree. The track is beautiful but maddeningly shapeless.

Season of Lights... Laura Nyro in Concert (1977)

Personnel:
Laura Nyro: vocals, piano, acoustic guitar
John Tropea: electric guitar
Richard Davis: double bass
Andy Newmark: drums
Carter C.C. Collins: percussion
Nydia 'Liberty' Mata: congas, percussion
Michael Mainieri: vibraphone, baliphone, clavinet
Jeanie Fineberg: flute, saxophone
Jeff King: saxophone
Ellen Seeling: trumpet
Recorded at Carnegie Hall, University of Colorado at Boulder, Massachusetts
outdoors, and Oakland
Musical direction: Laura Nyro
Location recording: Dale Ashby
Mix engineers: Don Puluse and Ron Johnsen
Label: Columbia
Release dates (Original single LP version): June 1977 (US), August 1977 (UK)
Chart places: US: 137
Running time: 69:39 (2-LP version)
Current edition: Iconoclassic 2008 CD

The marriage to David Bianchini, which had begun with bright-eyed optimism, was not long-lived, and by 1976 divorce proceedings were under way. In spring of that year, Laura embarked on a four-month tour to promote *Smile*. For backing musicians, she recruited seasoned New York session players, including some who'd played on the *Smile* recordings, and added newcomers like flautist/saxophonist Jean Fineberg and trumpeter Ellen Seeling. For someone known for her idiosyncratic approach to tempo, the learning curve must have been steep. This was the first full-band tour of her career. In live performance, compromise was needed on both sides. Drummer Andy Newmark later told Laura's biographer, 'She tried to adapt to the band', while guitarist John Tropea's recollection was that 'We had to fit into Laura's rhythms'. Several of the concerts were recorded for a live album, and though the audiences are never less than enthusiastic, the compromises sometimes show, in arrangements that are tasteful but lacking in intensity. The difficulty may be that when a maverick like Laura is integrated into a full band, it brings her into the landing zone of less original talents, with results being more listener-friendly but less distinctive.

Columbia had originally intended a double-vinyl set consisting of 16 tracks, and that version was sent to some outlets as a promotional copy. For unknown reasons, the company got cold feet and instead released a single vinyl set of ten tracks only. This is a great shame, because the longer version – thankfully now available – has much more of a sense of continuity and restores the missing songs and instrumental jams edited out for the single-disc release. It must also have frustrated Laura, who had painstakingly chosen what she considered were the best versions of each song.

As well as overhauling the arrangements, Laura made a few minor lyric changes to her old repertoire. The most significant is in 'When I Was A Freeport', where 'I'm a woman waiting for due time' becomes 'I'm a woman/ *And this is my due time*', signalling a new feminist assertiveness in the mature artist. Curiously, this is one point where the sequencing of the truncated release is superior to that of the two-disc set. Laura punningly introduces 'Freeport' – a song about an ex-lover – with the words, 'This is a song about another cat' – clearly referring back to 'The Cat-Song'; one track should follow the other.

Though the hints were there on *Smile*, *Season of Lights* reveals Laura as even more of a jazz stylist than previously supposed. As several tracks dissolve into scat-singing, the spirit of Nina Simone and Sarah Vaughan never seems far away. Sometimes the fusion elements work very well – the vibes intro on 'I Am The Blues'; the flute roulades on 'Upstairs By A Chinese Lamp; the percussion soloing on 'Timer', and the innovative use of baliphone (a type of African xylophone). There are genuinely exciting performances here – a driving, funky treatment of 'Money' for instance, and a poised solo rendition of 'Emmie' – but while one values the live atmosphere and the sense that Laura is enjoying herself on the road, these are not necessarily the versions everyone will return to.

The album sleeve used paintings by Rokuro Taniuchi (1921-81), an acclaimed illustrator known for his surreal, childlike covers for the weekly magazine *Shūkan Shinchō*. Evidently, they'd caught Laura's fancy on her visits to Japan.

A couple of tracks are unique to the album…

'The Morning News'

This is a song she never recorded in the studio. Possibly she never finished it to her satisfaction. Reliant on a heavy two-chord piano vamp leavened by Michael Mainieri's vibraphone, it sounds like a lyric in search of musical embodiment. The causes increasingly dear to her heart are on parade – suspicion of the press, Native American rights, the unholy alliance between war and business that pundits call the military-industrial complex. The most interesting couplet expresses a disconnect between inner and outer: 'Two worlds spin in time/One around you and one inside'. Within herself, she strives to build a peaceable kingdom; beyond herself, she sees strife, injustice and discrimination.

'Mars'

The instrumental coda to 'Smile' now gets its own title. Reconceived for the touring band's instrumentation, it preserves the oriental feel despite the absence of Japanese timbres. This loose jam must be the closest approach to the spirit of free jazz on any Nyro album, and it's rather splendid. The spirit of Miles Davis' fusion experiments hovers in the air, also perhaps the afterglow of Weather Report's 1974 breakout album *Mysterious Traveller*.

What to make of the title? Was Laura interested in astrology? In concert, she was wont to say that as a Libra, she liked 'balance'. But that may be no more than the lighthearted interest of someone who checks her horoscope in the daily paper. The song 'Smile' has the lines 'Mars is a-risin'/Mars in the stars' and leads into this instrumental, now titled 'Mars'. Another song on the *Smile* album ('I Am The Blues') contains the line 'Maybe Mars has good news'. It's hard to see these as astrological references to herself. Mars isn't a planet that's influential on Libra. Mars in Libra is said to be 'in detriment' (where a planet is in the sign opposite to that which it rules.) Libra is ruled by Venus. ('All roads lead to Venus', she sings in the much later song 'Triple Goddess Twilight'.) In contrast, her husband David Bianchini was an Aries, a sign ruled by Mars. With his wartime background, he was also a veteran servant of Mars, the Bringer of War in Greek mythology. All these thoughts – or none of them – may play into the title.

Nested (1978)

Personnel:
Laura Nyro: vocals, electric and acoustic piano, church organ, guitar, string ensemble
Will Lee, Cyril Cianflone, Tony Levin: bass
Andy Newmark: drums
Vinnie Cusano, John Tropea: guitar
Nydia 'Liberty' Mata: percussion
John Sebastian: harmonica
Felix Cavaliere: electric piano, organ
Recorded at Dale Ashby's mobile recording unit, Danbury, Connecticut, spring 1978
Producers: Laura Nyro, Roscoe Harring
Engineers: Pop and Dale Ashby, Frank Koenig
Label: Columbia
Release dates: June 1978 (US), August 1978 (UK)
Chart places: US: Did not chart
Running time: 37:13
Current edition: Iconoclassic 2008 CD

Speaking to *Rolling Stone* during the *Season of Lights* tour, Laura was clear where her priorities lay from now on: 'Travelling around: it uproots you … One thing I take seriously is having a baby. That's part of my feminism. Now women think first. They see the full meaning of it, the responsibility of it'.

Her relationship with Greg Bennett was floundering, perhaps because he didn't share her desire for parenthood. At this point, a new man entered her life. Harindra Singh – known as Hari – was of Indian ancestry, the son of a raja allegedly, and by all accounts, something of a charmer. They bonded over a shared interest in Indian spiritual teaching. Soon after he came to stay in Danbury, Laura became pregnant. He seems to have been out of her life again by the time she was ready to give birth in summer 1978. The twin developments of her mother's death and anticipation of new life had prompted a fresh onrush of creativity. She had new songs and an urge to commit them to vinyl. A pregnant Laura was reluctant to commute to the New York studios, opting instead to record at home with a mobile truck. Production duties fell to her longtime road manager Roscoe Harring. She called up several players she'd worked with before, including guitarist John Tropea, bassist Will Lee and keyboardist Felix Cavaliere. (Another guitarist used on the project – Vinnie Cusano – would go on to greater things, sort of, when he joined the band Kiss under his new name Vinnie Vincent.)

The recording sessions were relaxed, slow and somewhat haphazard. As in her earlier sessions, she relied on fellow musicians who *believed* in her. She liked to warm up with a group sing-along of Motown favourites. Though those dense piano polychords continued to prove a challenge for a bass player searching for the root note, her style was growing simpler. The previous year's experience of touring with a band had its effect: gone were the crazy tempo changes and asymmetric structures. The new songs were more conventional in form, often falling into standard verse/chorus or verse/bridge shapes. The lyrics, too, were less opaque, reflecting homely concerns or her newfound alternative spirituality. The results are mellow, too mellow for some. Her voice, as always, is an instrument of unique expressiveness, but the inventive arrangements of earlier albums are absent, so that many of the tracks, as critic Peter Doggett has observed, exude 'the spontaneous innocence of demo recordings'.

Reviewers were divided on Laura's new sound. Paul Rambali in *New Musical Express* found the album 'uninspired' and a fall into 'chintzy domesticity and romantic slush that Ms. Nyro should never have come to'. In contrast, Britain's other big music weekly, *Melody Maker*, praised the 'balance of introspection and exuberant celebration' and noted a 'melodic authority and confidence' not heard since *Christmas and the Beads of Sweat*.

In the striking cover photo by Adger W. Cowans, Laura looks out at the viewer with a fixed gaze, a red flower in her hair. What is she thinking? Perhaps that she has left one life behind and is on the cusp of a new one. *Nested* is an album of transitions. The lyric sheet includes a poem, 'Wind Circles', which she seems to have never set to music: a shame, since it is superior to many of the album's lyrics. The poem feels like a valediction, addressed to someone: Greg Bennett, maybe, who supported himself 'through odd jobs/and maintenance'. Laura is travelling lost, but 'wind circles/send me home to myself' and 'this song/may be purely my own'. There will be no more men in her romantic life.

Columbia didn't exert themselves in promoting *Nested* on its initial release, and it was the first Nyro album to fail to break into the *Billboard* Top 200 chart. Long out of print, it reappeared on vinyl in a 2021 box set; it may yet win new friends.

'Mr. Blue (The Song Of Communications)' (Laura Nyro)

As if picking up where 'Midnite Blue' left off, this next album begins with another song probably inspired by her 'gypsy man' Greg Bennett. We seem to be at a later, less dewy-eyed point in the relationship, however, a point of decision – in this lyric, it's she who brought the 'gypsy fire' to their romance. Like a lot of men partnered with successful women, Bennett seems to have struggled with not being the breadwinner. There's a suggestion, too, that he didn't share Laura's wish to have a child. In the song, she hopes they can remain friends and end their conflicts, even if they can't mend the 'broken dishes' of their love. She tries out a variety of different techniques here – spoken word to suggest a long-distance call with her lover, and cod sci-fi imagery that is new to her work. The lovers have grown so far apart, it's as if one is on Earth and the other in 'outer space'. (Their relative positions seem to switch in the course of a none-too-coherent lyric.) All the while she's been expertly studying the radar, because – surprise, surprise – she's a 'fucking mad scientist too'. It's a playful call to keep the channels of communication open.

Constructed (like 'Midnite Blue') around a somnolent rocking between two guitar chords, the track is rescued from inertia by a sinuous vocal that rises above the instrumental wash. Her voice remains a thing of unique, expressive power. The question is, once the urgency of her early work is dissipated, what does it want to tell us?

'Rhythm And Blues' (Laura Nyro)

She's back in the party spirit of songs like 'Sweet Blindness' and 'Time And Love'. Her man – 'Mr. Fox' aka 'the blue fox' – is going to take her downtown, where they'll 'harmonise by starlight'. The mood is nostalgic, with a hint of forbidden love (Both 'Mama' and 'Daddy' advise her not to go). As she asks Mama for help in finding her silver shoes and perfume, perhaps she's thinking back to teenage dates. The association between music and sex is never far out of mind – 'Rock me, roll me, rhythm and blues', she sings, in anticipation of seeing Mr. Fox. Interestingly, the phrase 'country nights' reappears from 'Smile', although this time any salacious pun, if intended, isn't spelt out in the printed lyrics.

Musically, it's a jaunty barrelhouse rocker, less original in concept than her earlier feel-good songs but a pleasant enough way to spend three minutes. Predictable in form, the track's most distinctive feature is the louche harmonica-playing of The Lovin' Spoonful's John Sebastian. He and Laura shared a road manager in Roscoe Harring, and this connection frequently brought them together after Laura's move to Connecticut. A friendship formed, built on Sebastian's regard for her as an artist. 'I wasn't faint of heart when it came to being a fan of hers', he told John Stix later. 'I let her know that if she was going to have a harmonica, I bloody wanted to be the harmonica player'.

'My Innocence' (Laura Nyro)

'When I turned 30, my love songs changed from romantic notions to a deeper taste of life. My mother died right before I wrote the songs for *Nested*'. The words are Laura's, in conversation with Bruce Pollock in 1984. 'My Innocence' makes the point. What she calls her 'innocence' comes from her 'warm earth mother/Out along the gravestones'. In turn, she communicates this same quality to her 'cold, cold lover' – a man with 'Indian hair': a reference to either Hari Singh or Greg Bennett, who had American Indian ancestry. Whoever she's addressing, she can't find common ground with him: she looks for his hand, 'but it isn't there'. Her innocence is something ungovernable, a 'wild thing' carrying her to an 'unknown future'. That future of 'me and you' evidently includes a child – whether a hoped-for baby or the one she already carried in her body would depend on when the song was written.

It's an up-tempo guitar-led track, surprisingly breezy given the tone of some of the lyric, which canters towards the payoff in its final verse, a promise of new life that will complete a cycle. We are born of earth and return to earth; a mother bears a daughter; the daughter, in turn, may bear new life. That's a thought to keep in mind as the track ends with an extended instrumental coda, Cusano and Tropea trading licks. It sounds as if the musicians are enjoying each other's company; the ensemble tight, yet the atmosphere relaxed. After a couple of so-so opening tracks, this is where the album starts to take off.

'Crazy Love' (Laura Nyro)
The piano was absent from 'My Innocence'. In contrast, 'Crazy Love' is presented as a solo with piano, and it captures some of the raw intensity of Laura's live performances. A serpentine melody uncoils over stately chordal accompaniment (Do we hear a reminiscence of Erik Satie in those major sevenths?), climaxing with an impassioned delivery of the title phrase. It's another love song directed to her 'gypsy man': presumably the Ohio-born Bennett, who blew into her life 'from the Midwest plains and rivers'. Watching her through 'deer's eyes', he moves 'like an animal on silent feet', but this softness is combined with 'ways of steel'. The lyric poetically captures how contradictory qualities in a lover may inspire 'crazy love' in us. 'Why did you make me feel this need?' she asks, anguish in her voice. After all that's passed between them, she wonders if she ever knew him at all. Something causes her to ache behind his 'snake cold back', and the answer may lie in the phrase 'Father of my unborn star'. While it's tempting to apply this description to Hari Singh, the father of her future child, it could also refer to the breakup with Bennett and the child she wanted with him but didn't have – the never-born.

'American Dreamer' (Laura Nyro)
After several reflections on the trials of love, side one ends in angrier mode with a song that takes aim at a range of targets. Her commercial fallout with David Geffen – or perhaps the earlier parting from Artie Mogull –-seems to be still on her mind: she recalls a smiling manager and how she signed a 'strange contract' with 'transparent lines'. As 'autumn's child' (Laura was an October baby), she was too naïve when she signed on the dotted line. (With Geffen's help, she'd successfully sued to void her contract with Mogull, on the grounds that she'd entered into it in 1966 while still a minor.) Despoiled innocence could even be a subtext here – curiously, the manager has an illustration from a child's first reading book (*Spot and Jane*) on his desk. The doctors who tell a patient 'she's imagining things' may refer to her mother's late cancer diagnosis; likewise, the recurring line 'We could not get there in time'. Also in the cast are lawyers (never a popular breed in anyone's book) and 'cops and robbers'. However, personal and public concerns merge, collage-style, so it's a rash interpreter who tries to pin the lyric down. Having given us the flipside of the American dream and exposed her disillusionment, Laura recovers a measure of rosy optimism in the final verse. She's once again the 'American dreamer/Flyin' high'.

It's a simple arrangement built around Laura's Fender Rhodes – the Nested sessions were the first time she'd recorded with an instrument that would feature on numerous later recordings. The electric piano has none of the expressive or percussive potential of a concert grand, but it fits smoothly enough into the soft-rock vibe created here.

'Springblown' (Laura Nyro)
This simple love song which opens side two may date from Laura's romance with Hari Singh: the allusion 'seeds of our baby' points in that direction. It describes a time of quiet contentment when the mere sight of the lover's face is 'like a warm embrace'. She's waiting for something – perhaps impending birth – and, in its neatest turn, the lyric equates the passage of time with efflorescence: 'A rose is pressing/Through a clock on the wall'.

'Springblown' is one of several tracks here composed on guitar. Never keen to master a multiplicity of chord shapes, she would tune the guitar to an open chord, then was able to switch chord simply by fretting all the strings simultaneously with one finger. Such 'open tunings' were commonplace in folk-derived guitar styles in the 1960s, although Laura's contemporaries often handled them with more sophistication and variety (Joni Mitchell's 'Big Yellow Taxi' is a good example). A lead guitar (whether from Cusano or Tropea isn't clear from the liner notes) adds some blues-style bottleneck, enlivening this rather torpid exercise. 'All my life I'm searching for celestial harmony', she sings. It's hard to capture the music of the spheres, and, regrettably, this doesn't come close.

'The Sweet Sky' (Laura Nyro)
After the low-key play-out of 'Springblown', it's a pleasure to greet one of the album's strongest tracks. Laura has recovered the sky-rocket fizz of her youth. The mood is celebratory. Yes, she may still be 'mixed up like a teenager', exploding into the 'sweet sky' like a firecracker on the Fourth of July; yes, the old disregard for rules may still be there. But with maturity has come self-knowledge and openness – 'I'm free if I can be me'. And with self-knowledge comes openness, a non-judgmental realisation that 'people are beautiful'; indeed, rhythm itself is beautiful.

Appropriately for such a retrospective song, the texture is closer to the bouncy, commercial sound of her youth. With its irrepressible shuffle rhythm and fluent chord progression, it's a real earworm. Whether the presence of her old comrade Felix Cavaliere (who guests here on electric piano) has anything to do with this, is pure speculation. As the song draws to an end, there's even a delightful and unexpected coda where she multitracks harmony vocals to weave variations on the title words.

'Light-Pop's Principle' (Laura Nyro)
For *Nested* – as for *Season of Lights* – Laura and her people called on an on-location mobile recording service based in Basking Ridge, New Jersey, operated

by the father-and-son team of Bill and Dale Ashby. Bill (known as 'Pop') had a scientific background, and according to friend Patti DiLauria, Laura delighted in teasing out his knowledge. The result is this rather incoherent new-age-type lyric relating light and energy to mind stuff, the planetary soul and the unity of all creation: 'Pop' philosophy in every sense. Propelled by Laura's electric piano, it hastens on its way, redeemed only by some exquisite background harmonies.

'Child In A Universe' (Laura Nyro)

Compared to the previous track, this is a much more successful engagement with similar ideas, minus the undigested physics. Over three verses, she addresses three different heavenly bodies: a star, the sun and the moon. In the first, she recognises that, like the earth, she's part of a universal whole, 'a grain in the galaxy'. In the second, she acknowledges the great chain of being in which we take our place with planets above us and 'rocks and fish' under our feet. The third verse finds her seeking the moon's help, singing, 'Can we talk a while?'. She just can't cope. Maybe the moon can send some peace on Earth. 'Send it to a child of the universe'. The moon as presiding deity often features in Laura's work, and in a later song ('The Descent Of Luna Rosé') is linked explicitly to the menstrual cycle. Here she thinks rather of the child she's carrying – or hopes to carry (we can't be sure when the song was written). Nothing concentrates the mind like motherhood.

Musically, there's more going on. We open with ethereal synth strings – most likely an ARP Solina – hinting at the celestial realm we're about to enter. Once the piano and voice enter, the rhythm section drops in and out – perhaps suggesting, by means of alternating texture, the dialogue between earthbound and skybound. And we go out on Nydia Mata's percussion improvisation over a repeated piano motif. All this adds up to a resourceful response to an inventive lyric and makes 'Child In A Universe' one of the album's best tracks.

'The Nest' (Laura Nyro)

The album ends with Laura singing of her pregnancy. There's joy, tinged with trepidation. She's preparing a warm, safe place for her newborn, which causes her to identify with other nest-builders – birds collecting twigs for a home in the trees, the Eskimo mother pictured in a print on the wall who carries her baby in a papoose. Picturing herself as an earth mother, she imagines what is unfolding within her, and – like any woman approaching childbirth for the first time – feels anxiety ahead of the unknown: 'I'd like to know how to give and let live'.

It's another very simple arrangement that foregrounds Laura's meditative vocal. Though Felix Cavaliere returns to flesh out the texture with his unflashy organ-playing, the track has the feel of a demo in wait for a skilled arranger. It's a pity Cavaliere wasn't given a free hand to develop the material, since 'The Nest' makes for a decidedly mellow conclusion to an often-downbeat album.

However, as it stands, it represents an honest and sincere expression of subject matter rarely broached in popular music: the brooding quicksilver emotions of an expectant mother.

Contemporary Track
'Mama Roux' (Dr. John Creaux, Jessie Hill)

Released on *American Dreamer: Live at the Bottom Line, 12th July 1978* (CD, 2016)

At the club dates she played to promote *Nested* in 1978, Laura would often include this song as an encore.

Dr. John (real name Malcolm John Rebennack, Jr.) was someone Laura may well have seen in concert. He typically performed a lively, theatrical stage act inspired by medicine shows, Mardi Gras costumes and voodoo ceremonies, favouring elaborate costumes and headdress. 'Mama Roux' made its first appearance on his 1968 album *Gris-Gris*, an innovative hybrid of New Orleans R&B and psychedelic rock. The original version is a growling, bluesy, half-spoken/half-sung concoction accompanied by shakers, congas, timbales and assorted percussion, with organ pedals in lieu of bass guitar. Heaven knows what it's about. Mama Roux – 'Queen of the little red, white and blue' – issues vague death threats; there's a 'medicine man' up to no good, and we get steamy hints of sexual indiscretion. That's New Orleans for you. Maybe.

In her live recording (solo with piano), Laura teases the audience by suggesting she has nothing else prepared. A shouted request from the audience for 'I Never Meant To Hurt You' goes unanswered. 'What else did I practise?' she muses, fingers straying over the keys, before accelerating into this number, which she says she learned 'off an album'. It's a sultry and fun performance – the long round vowel of 'Roux' clearly appealed to her – which doesn't adhere too closely to the original lyrics. As ever in her cover versions, she's in the process of turning it into a song of her own.

Mother's Spiritual (1984)

Personnel:
Laura Nyro: vocals, harmonies, acoustic and electric pianos, dulcimer on 'Sophia'
Terry Silverlight: drums
Elysa Sunshine: bass
John K. Bristow: electric guitar
Todd Rundgren: synthesizer on 'Man In The Moon' and 'Trees Of The Ages'
Nydia 'Liberty' Mata: percussion
Jan Nigro: acoustic guitar
Julie Lyonn Lieberman: violin
Recorded at home studio, Danbury, Connecticut, autumn 1983
Producers: Laura Nyro, Roscoe Harring
Engineers: Roscoe Harring, Arthur Kelm, Chris Andersen
Label: Columbia
Release date: January 1984 (US)
Chart place: US: 182
Running time: 44:53
Current edition: Iconoclassic 2009 CD

Laura gave birth to a baby boy on 23 August 1978. She named him Gillian – in memory of her mother Gilda – but from childhood down to the present, he's generally been known as Gil. The next decade saw Laura devote much of her energy to his upbringing, and it was no surprise that motherhood emerged as the focus of her new songwriting. In a 1984 interview with Bruce Pollock, she described her approach:

> Most of the songs I wrote at night. I would just wake up in the middle of the night. I had a young baby, and that's when I found the space to write. I didn't work with a tape recorder. I would write my ideas down. I have love songs written upside-down on matchbook covers. I'd write on my hand if there was no paper. Subject-wise, I wanted to reflect a new world, because that's what I was feeling: the songs were just moments right out of my life.

The recording process was less than focused, with a couple of false starts before the final sessions. Originally she planned to record the album at her Danbury home, as she had *Nested*, and she spent nine months or so (spring to late-1982) developing demos at home. A band of sympathetic musicians helped out. True to her principles, she now wanted gender equality in her band, so drummer Terry Silverlight and guitarist John Bristow were complemented by new bassist Elysa Sunshine and percussionist Nydia Mata, the latter a regular collaborator since the early-1970s. Laura then found what seemed like the ideal location to complete the project: a studio known as The Boogie Hotel, on Long Island, New York. Old friend Joe Wissert was persuaded to commute from California to produce the sessions, but creative tensions emerged in the relationship, and again she wasn't happy with the results.

Finally, she decided to build a studio in her home, as opposed to using a mobile truck as she had for *Nested*. The 48-track facility – state of the art for its day – didn't come cheap, costing somewhere between $150,000 and $200,000. It hung within the frame of the house, to mask vibrations from aircraft passing overhead. From its triple-glazed isolation booth, she could sit at her piano and look out over the pond.

The musicians were summoned back, and by summer 1983, the new album was taking shape. One new recruit was violinist Julie Lyonn Lieberman. Laura had been drawn to the meditative quality of Lieberman's recording *Empathic Connections,* and encouraged her to layer multiple violin tracks, from which Laura handpicked the passages she wanted. Her road manager Roscoe Harring shared production duties with Laura: it was very much a homegrown project, reflecting the quieter, more sedate life she now led. For a while, Todd Rundgren was roped in as co-producer, but his efforts to push her towards a more commercial product were rebuffed. She knew what she wanted. Rundgren later gave interviewer John Stix an account of these sessions, which doesn't reflect well on either artist. Rundgren felt his male ego was bruised by a 'militantly feminist' atmosphere at the sessions. Laura's perfectionism led her to record take after take 'without any judgement being made about any of them'. An ardent admirer of her work since *Eli* (Rundgren's 1970 album *Runt* bears her influence, and the track 'Baby Let's Swing' explicitly name-checks her), he was disappointed to find she was now 'constantly going for one sort of monotonal emotional pitch'.

Mother's Spiritual was Laura's favourite of her albums. She told her friend Patty DiLauria that it was 'as close as possible to her artistic vision. It was near perfect. 95 per cent there'. Reading between the grooves, the LP is also a celebration of a new love: her relationship with artist Maria Desiderio, which began around this time and endured to the end of Laura's life. Every detail had to be right. For the inside cover art, she found Oregon-based artist Jo Hockenhull, who later recalled working on the commission *in situ* at Danbury, 'watching snow cover the birches, and listening to Laura at the piano'.

However, critical reaction was mixed, often within the same review. *Rolling Stone* liked her 'flamboyantly passionate voice' but found her tree-hugging songs 'downright cuckoo'. The *New York Times* applauded the 'organic musical style' and lovely 'pantheistic hymns', while bemoaning that she overlaid her ideas with 'an earnest but garbled feminist critique of the world'. Less forgiving, in his albums roundup, the *Village Voice*'s Robert Christgau sneered that the 'romantic generalisations of matrifocal ecofeminism' were especially suited to this artist's 'moody style of gush'. As the falling-out with Todd Rundgren demonstrates, Laura's new direction was testing the patience of erstwhile male fans. While *Mother's Spiritual* eloquently conveys her intensifying concern with feminism, if the album has a single theme, it is one pressing on any new parent: How do we make a better world in which to bring up our children?

One publication had no doubts about *Mother's Spiritual*. The alternative magazine *Woman of Power* described the album as 'one of the strongest feminist statements to come out on a major record label' and carried a lengthy interview with Laura in its spring 1985 issue. The interview – a kind of companion piece to the album – is the most detailed statement she ever made about what she was against (patriarchy, war, racism, sexism) and what she was for: matriarchy, children, nature, peace, spirituality. The topics are very prescient for the 21st century, even if the new-age-like expression sometimes grates. Feminism, she suggested, is a complement to mothering, because 'self-defined women bring a special kind of spirit to their children – a gift of honesty'. She continued:

> When I envision a feminist world, everything takes on a new meaning. Everything is redefined: from human rights, to architecture, to everyday imagery. Artists, women and children would have a voice in the world – so the world would have a soft curve to it. It would also be more fun.

Laura's percussionist friend Nydia Mata recalled that 'she was a kid at heart. She had the best giggle of anybody I know'. Much of *Mother's Spiritual* is in deadly earnest, but the sense of fun hasn't entirely deserted her. If not scaling the heights of her earlier work, it's nonetheless a feistier album than *Nested*.

'To A Child...' (Laura Nyro)

By subtitling the opening track 'Gil's Song', Laura nails her colours to the mast. This album is borne of the joys, discoveries and associated discontents of motherhood. At the outset, we meet her, tired but happy, a single mom in the park with a hyperactive toddler – or 'an elf on speed', as she calls him in a memorable phrase underscored by a chord change from G minor to G major. Vulnerable and searching for answers, she expects the two of them to grow side by side, each finding their own way in life. Magazines preach pieties about life after parenthood – 'Silent lies never give you what you need' – neglecting to warn you about those inevitable moments when you'll be 'crying by the washing machine'. Her own creativity may even take a knock: currently, she's 'a poet without a poem'. Yet such concerns dissolve in love of the newborn and her delight in watching him running and climbing. In the *Woman of Power* interview, she describes how, immersing herself in nature, her spirituality became very 'elfin': as if the tree spirits she will celebrate in later tracks, merge with the elfin vitality of her infant son.

A 'springy lullaby' is how Laura described the song in a note to herself headed 'Tempos'. After a pensive intro with piano alone, one of the richest of her later melodies unfolds inventively through a couple of key changes. Electric piano joins a discreet rhythm section. The voice is less strident than in earlier years. She avoids her upper register and at one or two points, allows the words to disappear into the mix altogether, thus losing some lyrics of *haiku*-like simplicity ('The park is late/The wind is long'). This is the one track Todd Rundgren lent his production assistance to. His account, given later to John Stix, encapsulates the uneasy role he played in the album's evolution:

> When I heard it, I had a vision of how I thought it should or could come out. I kind of prodded her just to get some takes and get an approach on it. Once we got something, she got equivocally satisfied with it. The idea of full satisfaction was never an aspect of the recording process when I was involved.

This strong opener is among the few of Laura's later songs to attract cover versions. On the 2014 tribute album *Map to the Treasure*, it finds a staunch advocate in Dianne Reeves, supported by jazzman Billy Childs' sumptuous new arrangement.

'The Right To Vote' (Laura Nyro)

Motherhood intensified Laura's interest in feminism, and this track threatens to veer off into the preachy mode that alienated some erstwhile fans. What saves it is a sense of humour. Elsewhere, she'll present her beliefs with a pious face, but here the tone feels more skittish, even self-deprecating. Sometimes, girls just wanna have fun. She's glad women have the right to vote but, faced with a choice between the loudmouth and the belligerent, there's no one worth voting for. Under the shield of 'Patriarchal great religions', it's men who push the buttons and start the wars. Meanwhile, women's place 'is to wait and serve', dieting themselves into agreeable shapes, placated with gifts of microwave ovens and mink coats. Laura's first instinct is to board a spaceship 'to carry me the hell out of here'. Her second, more practical, response is to get drunk. Indeed, according to Keith Decker, who regularly babysat Gil while Mom was busy, the song was written during a drunken *soirée* with some girlfriends. Its unadventurous melody has something of that improvised character; only in the bridge – added later – does it take wing, with guitar flourishes from jazz-fusion exponent John Bristow.

'A Wilderness' (Laura Nyro)

'Feminist mothers are like pioneers in a wilderness – pioneers in a new world', Laura told *Woman of Power* in 1985. There *is* a narrative arc to this album, albeit less subtle than any she devised for her great 1960s trilogy. 'A Wilderness' seems to pick up where 'To A Child' left off. Again, mother and child are journeying together 'through the changing seasons'. Each must preserve their individuality, their untrammelled originality – what she calls the 'wilderness' within Gil and the 'wildness' in herself. And again, the outside world is a constraint: 'Many people pass by/Caught up in roles and rules'. Maybe Laura has to go out and face that world; that's why she's 'puttin' on some warpaint'.

This could suggest makeup, or it could refer to a Jain Sherrard book she's known to have read, which proposed that parenting is a kind of 'warfare' unlike any other, 'because both sides have to win'.

The track ends with an overdubbed recording of toddler Gil. In a barely audible riff, he pretends he's a crocodile, poised to gobble up first his bed and then Laura herself. It's a slightly alarming fantasy, true to children's taste for the macabre. Although unusual for the period, later songwriters would often incorporate this sort of *found* material into their work: think of the various quotations from Kate Bush's infant son Bertie on Bush's 2005 album *Aerial*.

With this pleasant little song, Laura draws closer, for better or worse, to the sound world of the late 1970s and early 1980s. Check out Elysa Sunshine's funky bassline and the vague wash of Fender Rhodes piano and stereo-chorused guitar lapping around the middle verses. It won't be to everyone's taste, but it's a reminder that her ears remained open to the music around her, just as her antennae were tuned to pick up social developments beyond the Danbury idyll.

'Melody In The Sky' (Laura Nyro)
Possibly the first song to be inspired by Laura's growing feelings for Maria Desiderio, this track marks a shift in emphasis – no more gender-specific pronouns from now on; no more captains or devils incarnate. She's 'not looking for Miss or Mr. Right': this careful form of words allows the possibility of bisexuality without making any overt statement. (The printed lyrics actually have '*waiting* for', but on the recording, she sings '*looking* for'.) Though framed as a declaration of love, the song is at pains to recognise the lovers' independence: 'You've got your life/Your love/Your life/Your love/I've got mine', she sings. Throughout their time together, Laura and Maria usually maintained separate living spaces, with Maria keeping a separate studio. Laura's previous partners may have struggled with being a celebrity's significant other. Maria – already established as an artist in her own right – seems to have forged a relationship of equals with her more famous partner. As ever, Laura comes up with a telling phrase to capture the distinct taste of being in love: here it's the 'sweet spicy waves' that overcome her.

Spirited, featuring hard-edged guitar, the track evokes the exhilaration of romance with some fine dramatic contrasts, especially in the bridge. But disappointingly, like several tracks on the album, 'Melody In The Sky' ends just as it's starting to go somewhere different and potentially interesting – in this case, with an instrumental jam between bass and guitar in the free-form spirit last encountered on *Season of Lights*. This is where a sharp-eared outside producer might have pulled the whole thing together in ways not obvious to those making the music. In a 1984 interview, Laura told Bruce Pollock that when she wrote the song, she heard 'gypsy violins'. Now, that could have been a mistake, thankfully swerved: in her many iterations of the love-song formula, Laura reliably avoided cliché.

'Late For Love' (Laura Nyro)

A different kind of love song, one addressed as much to herself as to any external lover. The idea seems to be that we don't have to go looking for love: it will find us. We search for it in the movies, by venturing on exotic adventures like pearl-diving, but 'love is where you are'. It's not a product manufactured in Japan (at that time, the workshop of the world, the role that China has since assumed). Nor is it to be confused with sex. The essential is to not be slow in recognising it when it comes along: 'Am I late for love?/ No, I can't be late for love'. She offered a gloss on this song in her *Woman of Power* interview:

> Certain primal experiences in my life – like birth and death – led me lyrically to a song I wrote called 'Late For Love'. After writing the song, I realised that it was made up of all questions, with some new answers. That song carries my spirituality: not a religion that's handed to you, but a personal meaning.

There's a touch of Burt Bacharach about this track, especially in the chorus (Laura was an admirer and recorded a couple of his songs towards the end of her life): a mellifluous, fluent lyricism that suits the subject matter well. As elsewhere on this album, the gloopy arrangement sometimes submerges the vocal, which is regrettable because her voice remains the one feature that elevates indifferent material to majestic heights.

'A Free Thinker' (Laura Nyro)

With electric piano dominating a tight jazz/funk groove, the in-your-face style seems all of a piece with what she wants to tell us here. Laura wears her feminism on her sleeve in this track. What might once have been wrapped up in enigma, is now baldly stated – women are expected to live through others, to 'play it demure', to be good consumers, to hide behind masks and conceal their true feelings. Better they should think for themselves, find their own style. That way, 'with some individuality', they 'may feel more alive'. All this is true and well said, but perhaps better said in a speech than a song. (A commentator risks the wrath of Nyro fans by suggesting as much, but he pleads in defence the verdict of her biographer, Michele Kort. Even Kort, who was deeply in tune with Laura's feminist concerns, regretted seeing her subject 'trade her once-elusive poetry for over-specific didacticism'.) One ominous sign is that – for the first time – Laura found it necessary to footnote her printed lyrics. An asterisk against the word 'hawks' in the final verse informs us that 'This word is being used in its traditional sense of war consciousness, and not in reference to the spirit of the soaring bird'.

'Man In The Moon' (Laura Nyro)

A beautiful melody calls forth a sultry vocal from Laura. Add in Todd Rundgren's moody synthesizer contributions, and 'Man In The Moon', which closes side one, is one of the album's standout tracks. It comes from a deep place, as Laura told Bruce Pollock in 1984:

> When I was very young, I remember sitting at a piano and hearing the notes and the chords ring out in the air, and I knew there was something special in that sound: some kind of freedom. More recently, when I was writing 'Man In The Moon' one night, as I was working through the chords, I remember getting the same feeling.

In the *Woman of Power* interview, Laura describes the moon and the stars as her 'wild romantic home'. In the album's cover photo, a striking monochrome image by Irene Young, Laura sports a prominent moon necklace. The full moon holds a fascination for every culture, and moon worship is a common feature of ancient religions. Many world mythologies recount stories of a 'man in the moon' whose face seems to look down at us from the moon's surface when it is full. This song plays around with the notion. The lyric suggests that Laura used to be in thrall to the moon man, but now realises that he simply embodied her fantasy for a 'new world' outside herself. She doubts that they really shared anything: he never knew the depth of her need or her prayer. Rather, the new world where she plans to raise children is *within* her. 'You know you're the old world and I'm the new world', she tells him emphatically in the final verse. Perhaps this man in the moon stands in for all the men in her life hitherto. With its demand for 'love, respect and power', the track articulates Laura's feminist, woman-oriented sensibility with a lot more subtlety than 'A Free Thinker'. In 1997, her friend Zoe Nicholson told the *New York Times* that, for Laura, 'Everything was about female energy – with the exception of her son – Mother Earth, Mother Nature, looking to the moon'.

This song went through some rewriting before finding its final berth on *Mother's Spiritual*. Laura performed an earlier version at the Bottom Line, New York, in July 1978, which is preserved on the recording of that show (and included as a bonus track on the 2009 CD reissue of *Mother's Spiritual*). Moonlight appears to be the controlling image in the original lyric, as she returns again and again to the line 'You lit up my love with yours'. The man in the moon was treated less respectfully at this stage – a reference to the dish running away with the spoon implied that he was no more than a figure from a nursery rhyme.

'Talk To A Green Tree' (Laura Nyro)
The majority of tracks on *Mother's Spiritual* are slow to medium-tempo ballads. Flip the record over, however, and side two opens on this up-tempo number with stylish guitar flourishes. Laura is really rocking out here. She told *Woman of Power* that the song was about 'talking to some higher spirit when you feel trapped in a draining situation'.

The subject matter returns us to the trials and obligations of motherhood. Laura is a 'working woman' with a baby on her back. She regrets that her own mother died before Gil was born. It'll be a tough row to hoe: she must teach her baby 'that love is what life is for' when all the world around her 'is still in love with war'. She invites a man to take her place and see how he copes with the domestic round 'eight days a week'. Ignored by deaf human ears, she's 'gonna talk to a green tree'. Lying by the tree with her infant, enjoying some quality arboreal 'company', she hopes to recoup her energy and set her spirit free.

It would be easy to mock all this as so much tree-hugging flapdoodle, were it not done with sincerity and a spice of humour.

'Trees Of The Ages' (Laura Nyro)

Mother's Spiritual carries a dedication on the sleeve: not to a person, but 'to the trees'. The house at Danbury was surrounded by woods. This second *tree* song celebrates the spirit of the trees that must've seemed like friends to Laura as she greeted them. A 'tangible reality of peaceful coexistence' is how she described her leafy chums in the *Woman of Power* interview. Trees will outlast us; their knowledge surpasses even that of Zen masters; they are protected by 'tree elves' who repair what people break. The lyric has a poetic beauty, particularly the opening image of the trees as they 'toss, shimmer in the wind'. It's good to know she's at one with the natural world and its biorhythms – 'energy spirals' as she calls them – but pantheism can induce a state of vegetative inertia. Slower than the previous track and rhythmically slacker, this exercise in tree-worship might come across as a tad po-faced. But the vibe seems right for the subject. A delicate synthesizer scale, ascending and descending on a sequence, fades in and out: a reminder that we're into the era of 1980s electronica.

'The Brighter Song' (Laura Nyro)

The 1970s and 1980s were a fruitful period in the women's movement. New currents of thought emerged. One branch – ecofeminism – related the oppression and domination of all marginalised groups, including women, to the oppression and domination of nature. Ecofeminists asserted that capitalism was just a reflection of paternal and patriarchal values. They argued that capitalism hasn't benefited women and has led to a harmful split between nature and culture, a split that can only be healed by the feminine instinct for nurture and holistic knowledge of nature's processes.

Laura was reading widely at the time, and – as the 1985 interview with *Woman of Power* shows – had clearly encountered these ideas. 'The Brighter Song' is addressed to a 'sister' who shares Laura's ecofeminist convictions, someone who does 'understand' the earth and wants an end to violence. 'You are a green peace dreamer', she sings, seeming to address not so much an individual as the sisterhood in general. It's an inclusive, comprehensive vision, allowing room for young and old, black and white. Once again, the moon is a presiding deity: the moon will shine a little brighter if the sister can only 'believe' in her happiness.

True to the title, this catchy little anthem gets a bouncy treatment from the supporting band. You might want to sing along. Or you might think this is a disappointing return to the polemical tone of 'A Free Thinker' and move on to the next track.

'Roadnotes' (Laura Nyro)

This song was reportedly written at Hilton Head Island in South Carolina, where Laura rented a house on the beach for a month. It's an evocation of life on the road, though perhaps recalling vacation road trips rather than musical tours. Staying in motels or camping in trailers, Laura assuages her 'gypsy fever' ('Gypsy' was a nickname for the RV they travelled in). She has child and dog with her, and celebrates a significant birthday while travelling. The only missing element is her 'angel of the night', her lover: 'I want everything that you can bring/To set the night in motion'. The lover's gender isn't specified, but one suspects that this erotically charged lyric is addressed to another woman. 'My love is the ocean', she sings – it's a revealing line. Like other women artists and songwriters, she turns instinctively to oceanic imagery. As pioneering feminist writer Hélène Cixous argued, the ocean is a metaphor for female subjectivity. Unlike the masculine trait of fortifying the self against invasion, female consciousness oozes out beyond the self to embrace the world.

Here Laura delivers the most seductive vocal anywhere on the album, soaring into her upper register for the word 'lover'. From its beginnings in attractive electric piano figuration, the arrangement builds satisfyingly in intensity, making this one of the album's strongest tracks.

'Sophia' (Laura Nyro)

Visitors to Danbury were surprised to find Laura living in relatively spartan circumstances amid simple furnishings. Though she was comfortably off, hers was not a life of conspicuous consumption. This song conveys that. She has no need of 'pretty things' or 'diamond rings'. Instead, she's looking for the 'highway' to her soul, hoping for enlightenment and guidance from two female deities. With their help, women may yet 'change the world'.

'Sophia' was the personification of wisdom in Greek religion. Like so much from the ancient world, her cult was carried over into Christian thinking, where she resurfaced as the word of God or an embodiment of the Holy Spirit. By the 1960s, Sophia was being reinvoked by neo-pagans who put her centre-stage in feminist spirituality. While never an adherent of Wicca or alternative religions in any practical way, Laura was drawn to these currents of thought. As she said in the *Woman of Power* interview, 'Goddess is the only lusty joyful spirituality I know of that empowers feminism'. Hecate – the other goddess addressed in this lyric – is also of Greek origin. She's variously associated with crossroads, entrances, night, light, magic, witchcraft, knowledge of herbs and poisonous plants, ghosts, necromancy and sorcery. Visually, Hecate was often represented in triple form and identified with the phases of the moon: new, waxing and full. (Laura kept these aspects in mind when she revisited such themes in the later song 'Triple Goddess Twilight'.) If evidence were needed that Laura has taken Hecate to heart and personalised her, it's striking that she insisted on pronouncing the name with a soft 'c' ('He*ss*ate', not 'Hekate'), despite being told this was incorrect.

At 4:39 in length, 'Sophia' is the longest track on *Mother's Spiritual*, ending with an extended instrumental break that features Laura's brother Jan on guitar. Powered by an abrasive funk riff, it features one of the album's most impassioned vocals. However abstract the subject matter might appear to some, Laura was very much in the moment here.

'Mother's Spiritual' (Laura Nyro)
One of her finest songs, the title track carries the dedication 'For my mother'. Becoming a mother herself had intensified Laura's sense of loss after her own mother's premature death. The phrase 'mother's spiritual' is teasingly ambiguous, bringing Laura's newfound interest in spirituality together with a conviction that her mother lived on *in spirit* – perhaps also referencing an African-American genre, the spiritual, that was among Laura's influences.

At the outset, thoughts of childhood crowd in. The opening lines, evoking a street corner 'where the kids boogie all night', may recall teenage years singing doo-wop with friends. A 'band of angels' who bring salvation suggest the protective warmth of family. As in 'Roadnotes', the ocean laps at her feet, singing to her 'that love is always alive'. It's interesting how each verse repeats the line 'she is the mother of time'. In Hinduism, Kali – one of the ten tantric goddesses – is the 'mother of time': something that Laura may have known, given her interest in Asiatic religions. Kali annihilates the ego which fuels the illusion of separation; when we die, our consciousness merges with her. The song speaks of a continuum of life, of 'rivers that give', of mothers who give birth.

The arrangement couldn't be simpler – voice supported by acoustic piano and violin – and is perfect for this visceral affirmation of contented domesticity. It's not the zany Laura of the 1960s, alas. But we all have to grow up sometime.

'Refrain' (Laura Nyro)
After the high of 'Mother's Spiritual', comes this brief and rather pointless coda. Over gurgling baby sounds (Gil, presumably), we get a reprise of three lines from 'To A Child', and one line from 'Late For Love'. She should've quit while she was ahead.

Contemporary Tracks
'Polonaise' (Jan Nigro)
Limited release as a single A-side, 1983 (US), b/w 'And That You Understand'
Kenny Rankin was a New York-born singer-songwriter who'd been around the music business since the early-1960s. He played guitar on Bob Dylan's

1965 album *Bringing It All Back Home* and had seen three albums of his own enter the *Billboard* chart. He got to know Laura later in the decade. Although her brother Jan never matched his sister's success, he is also a songwriter. 'Polonaise' was one of a number of songs he sent out speculatively to artists. Rankin picked this one up and elected to record it as a duet with Laura. With production in the hands of Patrick Williams and Hank Cicalo (the engineer on *Tapestry* and other Carole King albums of the 1970s), 'Polonaise' could've been a winner, and though promo copies were pressed (and now change hands for tidy sums on the secondhand market), the small record company behind it went bankrupt before the single received a general release.

The polonaise is a dance in 3/4 time, of Polish origin, Chopin's 20-plus polonaises for piano being probably the most famous examples. However, that's not the form of this slow, smoochy ballad. 'Polonaise' here seems to be a girl's name: 'When she sees the world as hunger/She feeds it with her smile/And she knows my secrets though I never say'. Rankin's smooth lounge delivery won't be to everyone's taste, but Laura's finely nuanced vocal rescues the song from sentimental overload.

The composer is mistakenly credited as '*Jon* Nigro' on the label.

'Creepin'' (Stevie Wonder)
Released on the CD accompanying the songbook *Time and Love: The Art and Soul of Laura Nyro* (2002)
Laura was a huge Stevie Wonder fan. In April 1970, the trade magazine *Cashbox* reported a visit she made to him between his shows at New York's Copacabana nightclub, with an accompanying photo showing her holding a dove to his ear. The admiration was mutual. In the same month, the Motown star told Don Heckman of the *New York Times*: 'I dig Laura Nyro very much. Also, I think she's cute. We write similarly in some ways; our chord structures are similar. And the sister sign of Taurus is Libra: she's a Libra and I'm a Taurus'.

This track – her little act of homage – came some years later. It was laid down with the *Mother's Spiritual* band in 1983 but never released at the time. An affectionate cover that sticks quite closely to the original (except for some chord substitutions and a melodic deviation on the line 'Why must it be…?'), it makes effective use of dulcimer, an instrument Laura occasionally reached for.

'Did John Sebastian tell you he played harmonica on a Stevie Wonder tune? She killed that!' – thus exclaimed Laura's sound engineer and road manager, Roscoe Harring, in an interview with John Stix. But there's no harmonica on the track as preserved. Perhaps Sebastian baulked at the prospect of trying to rival the harmonica solo on Stevie Wonder's original, which appeared on his 1974 album *Fulfillingness' First Finale*.

Laura: Laura Nyro Live at the Bottom Line (1989)

Personnel:
Laura Nyro: vocals, keyboards
Jimmy Vivino: guitar, electric mandolin, harmony vocals
David Wofford: bass
Frank Pagano: drums, harmony vocals
Nydia 'Liberty' Mata: percussion
Diane Wilson: harmony vocals
Recorded at The Bottom Line, New York City, summer 1988
Producers: Laura Nyro, Jimmy Vivino
Engineer: Mark Linett
Label: Cypress
Release date: October 1989 (US)
Chart place: Did not chart
Running time: 61:58
Current edition: Cypress 1989 CD

By 1988, Laura had been away from the stage for ten years. She'd concentrated on raising her son, consolidating relationships, travelling, and deepening her commitment to the causes she espoused. But she was still writing and keen to share with her public again. True to her principles, she put together a gender-balanced touring band: including herself it was three men and three women. The most influential new recruit was New-Jersey-born guitarist Jimmy Vivino, a friend of Felix Cavaliere. Like everyone joining the team, he had to adjust to Laura's working methods. All visionary artists have their idiosyncrasies. Drummer Bill Bruford recalled that when he joined English prog rock band King Crimson, rather than musical instruction, leader Robert Fripp gave him a reading list. At Vivino's first meeting with Laura, she handed him some notes written on a paper plate that started from the centre and continued circling outwards in a spiral towards the edges. 'They were just thoughts about the music, about songs, about what we were going to do', he told John Stix later. 'I thought that was inspired'.

With no product from Laura – one of their prestige artists – since 1984, Columbia wanted a new studio album and offered a generous recording budget. Laura's instinct, however, was to put out a live album. As she explained to Bill Flanagan of *Musician* magazine, she preferred the warmth and spontaneity of a live record: 'I don't feel much of that when working on a studio record unless everything goes very, very smoothly and quickly'. Her ideal was something akin to John Coltrane's 1962 disc *Live at the Village Vanguard*. At her own expense, she recorded a number of shows at The Bottom Line, a 400-seat venue in Greenwich Village, in summer 1988. When Columbia declined to put out the live album, her new manager David Bendett negotiated a one-off deal allowing her to release the live album with another label and then return to Columbia for her next studio offering. A deal was done with independent label Cypress Records to issue a double LP culled from the Bottom Line shows. However, without the backing of a major company, commercial success was elusive, even after she reportedly paid $18,000 for a quarter-page black-and-white advertisement in *Rolling Stone* magazine. But mixed reviews did nothing to dent Laura's faith in the record. In a radio interview shortly after its release, Ed Sciaky kept trying to pitch questions about her early work, which he clearly preferred. She brought him back firmly to *Live at the Bottom Line*: 'It tells you where I'm coming from right now as a writer, what's on my mind. And it draws from way back to when I was a teenager. And so it's got a lifeline'.

When musicians are conscious of the tape rolling, it can change a performance. But at these shows, so much was taped that the players relaxed and forgot they were being recorded. Under Vivino's leadership, the band sound tight and focused, without being *up*tight. As released, the album preserves plenty of audience reaction, and is testimony to how much love Laura still inspired. For her part, she appears more at ease than on some earlier live recordings – decidedly more chatty. This may be because she'd switched to playing electric keyboards instead of grand piano, enabling her to face the audience when performing.

In the setlist, a few songs survived from her early repertoire, but Laura insisted on new arrangements to keep the songs fresh. Seven tracks are unique to this album...

'High-Heeled Sneakers' (Robert Higginbotham)
'High Heeled Sneakers' (originally 'Hi-Heel Sneakers'), a 12-bar blues that was a chart success for Robert Higginbotham in 1964 under his stage name Tommy Tucker, had already been covered by countless artists from Elvis Presley and Tina Turner to Big Brother and the Holding Company. Apparently, Tucker had put in time as a competitive amateur boxer in the 1950s, which may lie behind the lyric's instruction to 'Wear some boxin' gloves/In case some fool might wanna fight'.

Laura and the band segue straight into this one from their opening number, 'The Confession', keeping the same up-tempo feel. On guitar, Vivino weighs in with lively blues licks. In Tucker's original, it was a man telling his woman to 'put on your red dress, baby/'Cause we're goin' out tonight'; Laura substitutes 'mama' for 'baby'. Liberated by her 'confession', is she now free to address another woman in erotic terms? Or is someone addressing her, now that she's a 'mama' herself?

'Roll Of The Ocean' (Laura Nyro)
Before settling on the live album concept, Laura laid down some home recordings at Danbury with bassist Chuck Rainey (a veteran of the 1968 *Eli* sessions) and drummer Steve Gadd. This was one of the songs they attempted. Back then, it wasn't completed to Laura's satisfaction. However, in presenting

the new band arrangement, she was careful on the sleeve of *Live at the Bottom Line* to credit Rainey and Gadd's earlier contribution. According to Jimmy Vivino, the touring band learned the song from the earlier recording: 'That original version of 'Roll Of The Ocean' – which I've never heard put out – was one of the greatest things I ever heard', he later told interviewer John Stix. 'We never approached the heaviness of that version'.

Heavy or not, in its final form on the live album, the song is a powerful statement of Laura's sense of connection to nature and the cosmos. As in 'Roadnotes', the ocean is identified with femininity: 'I'm a woman/I want the roll/The roll of the ocean'. This is a special category of desire: to be freed 'from a world that is so very hard and cold' and enter into a visionary realm that privileges flux and fluidity. She aspires to feel the 'sweet complete elemental roll' of a medium where we become buoyant, to merge into the aqueous womb from which our ancestors evolved millennia ago.

Fittingly for a track that mentions John Coltrane by name, this gets a jazz-like treatment. Laura delivers the first verse almost in rap style, before unfurling the melody as she sings of a 'starry aching tune'. Her voice has rarely sounded stronger than in this impassioned performance. The percussion battery is put to good use, too, with effective cymbal panning from left to right to suggest the ocean. Some clap-happies in the audience jump the gun, thinking it's all over at 2:51. Fortunately, it isn't: she continues with a soulful reprise for another minute and a half.

'Companion' (Laura Nyro)
Speaking to Bill Flanagan of *Musician* magazine in 1989, Laura described how her attitude to relationships had changed, and with it, her songwriting:

> Well, you know, I tell you, I put a lot of energy into writing about the male/female dance. Any men who are my friends now, I choose as human beings that I like, really get along with and can have a decent friendship with. But that came with maturity. Now the things that I'm writing about that involve women and men are kind of *our world*. That's pretty universal. My sight turned toward a certain kind of vision and interest in the world. It just crept into the songs. The song 'Companion' says that as far as love goes, it's a warm companion that I want. When I was very young, I was looking for trouble. I didn't know I was. But now I have too many important things to do; I don't want to be drained and I don't want trouble.

This simple love song expresses a simple conviction. She's not looking to marry again; she's financially independent. And while there's still room in her heart for 'a very special lust', what she seeks in middle age is companionship founded on 'a very special trust'. Laura sounds relaxed by this point in the set. Never very talkative between numbers, she teases the audience by prefacing this one with the words, 'And now that you're finally my captive audience,

I'm gonna force some more new songs on you'. As she introduces the band, she singles out Diane Wilson for supplying 'extra special harmonies' – the added vocal texture certainly enhances this slow, wistful ballad. But as ever, it's Laura's lead vocal that strikes home – the unexpected climb into her upper register for the bridge and again, very appropriately, for the line 'like a bird born to sing'. These are the dramatic touches that distinguish a great interpreter from a mediocrity.

'The Wild World' (Laura Nyro)

This song – and indeed the whole 1988 tour – was dedicated to the animal rights movement, which Laura had become interested in after one day chancing on a street stall set up by protestors. She saw a connection here to the civil rights and women's movements. Having become aware that her own living habits were contributing to animal suffering, she gradually stopped using products made with animal ingredients, and became a vegetarian. As she told Mark Sommer in a 1989 interview: 'I really had to educate myself and make a commitment, because I was one of those people who kind of enjoyed all that food!'. Her beloved grandfather had been a vegetarian, unusually for his time. However, she wasn't going to impose her views on her son – he must make up his own mind and decide how to spend his school lunch money. 'I remember that when I was becoming aware of the origins of food and clothing and things that were bringing about the extinction of animals, I couldn't sleep for a couple of nights', she told Sommer.

'The Wild World' sets all this to music, with references to wearing fur, animal experimentation, vegetarianism, and the slaughtering of animals in the wild. The opening lines capture her gastronomic delight at the prospect of 'Dinner in the kitchen/Delicious to eat'. Some old pleasures must be foregone, alas. Her mantra now is to 'Let wild things run free', to evade 'consumer blindness' and instead 'consider compassion'. In a 1989 radio interview, Scott Simon asked Laura why she began the song not with the wolf or the baby harp seal, but with food on a plate. She answered, 'You know, if everybody in some way could personalise it a little bit, it would make the situation for animals much more decent'. These are noble sentiments. Whether they make for great art, when so directly expressed, is an open question. Still, it's a hard-driving musical arrangement, with sharp guitar-noodling from Vivino and tight harmony vocals on the title line. As protest songs go, it succeeds in conveying righteous indignation without descending into agitprop. In fact, although not among the best tracks on the album, it's rather good.

'Park Song' (Laura Nyro)

We're back in the landscape of 'To A Child'. Laura and Gil are outdoors, in the park, where autumn leaves 'drift by like angels'. Where others might see the leaves as a symbol of fragility or transience, she views them as a source of strength, and addresses them in song. The lyric contrasts the unstructured simplicity of nature with the alleged greatness of 'man-made reality'. As often happens in her songs of this period, the link between these two worlds is the child – perhaps because, in the passage from innocence to experience, a child's socialisation mirrors our collective progress from nature to culture. Much may be lost in the process, she seems to be saying – we've ended up with a 'whole crazy world' – but delight in small things, like a child's love, redeems us.

These worthy thoughts call forth another sinuous melody; and the positive impression she wants to leave us with is reinforced by delicious harmony vocals, especially on the final line 'As you float down in wonder'.

'Women Of The One World' (Laura Nyro)
When Laura was a child, her mother took a job as a bookkeeper. 'The numbers kept her mind calm from the stresses of life' is how Laura described it in her 1989 radio interview with Scott Simon. This memory crept into the lyric here, with its reference to 'dancers, sweepers, bookkeepers'. She told Simon the song is a 'feminist vision' of the 'everydayness' of motherhood – that place where 'both sides of life meet', where 'taking-the-child-out-to-the-movies meets the mystic'. Beyond that, vaulting in familiar style from the particular to the general, the lyric calls on women across the world to unite in opposition to war. In what may be an earlier draft (reproduced in manuscript in *Lyrics and Reminiscences*), she makes the connection between motherhood and pacifism even more explicit – 'We bore you to live not die', she writes, as she wishes goodnight to the 'children of Nicaragua/And all through South Africa'.

At something under two minutes, this is the album's shortest track. It feels undeveloped and a touch sanctimonious, despite some exquisite vocal harmonising between Laura and Diane Wilson. At the end, it's as if the priestess, having delivered her brief sermon, steps down from the pulpit. 'That's our hit', she tells the audience mischievously, as the applause dies down.

'The Japanese Restaurant Song' (Laura Nyro)
Laura loved playing this song on tour. 'She had fun with that every night', her guitarist Jimmy Vivino recalled in a later interview. And it *is* a fun song, a pleasing relief from the slogan-heavy tracks elsewhere on this album – a snatch of 'day in the life' reportage, or a 'strange' song about 'family life', as she introduces it on the recording. It brings together her love of food and wine, her passion for the Orient, and the simple pleasures of partying. She visits a Japanese restaurant, with dogs and kids in tow, meets her lover, imagines what it would be like to be a geisha (though taking care not to forfeit her 'radical feminist bent'), and spars with the chef about the children's bad behaviour. Earlier in the day, we learn, she'd taken in a movie: a foreign film in black and white. (At one performance, she joked to the audience that she took acting lessons from old Anna Magnani movies. She was a great admirer of the Italian actress and especially loved *The Rose Tattoo*, the 1955 film scripted by Tennessee Williams, which netted Magnani her only Oscar.)

Laura's proudest claim at this time was that she'd finally given up cigarettes. As someone who'd smoked a pack a day since she was 15 – so she told Stephen Holden of the *New York Times* – she was delighted to find she could now hold her notes for twice as long. Every performance of 'The Japanese Restaurant Song' ended with an improvised rap where she told the imagined waitress how she'd just quit smoking and it had left her '*very* hungry'. She then ordered something. The order changed from night to night: on the *Bottom Line* album, it's 'a great big bowl of chocolate ice cream'. All the while, she'd fan herself with a Japanese paper fan. It was good theatre, and we can hear the audience's enthusiasm – which is just as well, because musically, the song is unremarkable, never developing much beyond a simple three-chord vamp. 'I'm trying to come at my writing more through the singing and the vocal line', she told interviewer Stephen Holden in 1989. For those of us who valued her inventive piano harmonies, this wasn't entirely welcome news.

Contemporary Track
'Let It Be Me' (Gilbert Bécaud, Manny Kurtz)/'The Christmas Song' (Mel Tormé, Robert Wells)
Released on the compilation album *Acoustic Christmas* (Various artists, 1990)
After a performance in Santa Monica, singer Natalie Cole visited Laura backstage and invited her to contribute to a benefit album to be released during the Christmas holiday season. Laura came up with this festive medley, combining a song made famous by The Everly Brothers in 1959 with another associated with Natalie Cole's father Nat King Cole. The two make an effective pairing, and Laura delivers them with concentrated intensity in a recording that deserved to be more widely available. It would provide a blessed relief from Yuletide standards like Mariah Carey's 'All I Want For Christmas Is You'.

This medley was also released as a cassette single, backed with Shawn Colvin's rendition of the Judy Garland classic from *Meet Me in St Louis* 'Have Yourself A Merry Little Christmas'. Laura re-recorded 'Let It Be Me' in 1994 for an album project of her own, a version that appeared posthumously on *Angel in the Dark*.

Walk the Dog & Light the Light (1993)

Personnel:

Laura Nyro: lead vocals, harmonies, keyboards

Bernard Purdie: drums

Freddie Washington: bass

Jerry Jemmott: bass on 'Walk the Dog & Light the Light'

Elliott Randall, Michael Landau, Ira Siegel: guitar

Bashiri Johnson, Erik McKain: percussion

Ellen Uryevick: harp

Juliet Haffner, Sue Pray, Julie Green, Jeanne Le Blanc, Marilyn Wright, Belinda Whitney Barratt, Joyce Hammann, Beryl Diamond, Rani Vaz, Laura Seaton, Gene Orloff, Sanford Allen, Mindy Jostyn: strings

Lou Marini, Roger Rosenberg, Randy Brecker, Lawrence Feldman: horns

Michael Brecker: saxophone solo

Lou Marini: flute solo

Laura Nyro, Carlos Franzetti: string arrangements

David Frank: horn and flute arrangements; additional production assistance

Recorded atRiver Sound Studios, 95th Street, New York City, summer 1993

Producers: Gary Katz, Laura Nyro

Engineer: Wayne Yurgelun

Label: Columbia

Release dates: September 1993 (US), January 1994 (UK)

Chart place: Did not chart

Running time: 36:17

Current edition: Sony/Columbia 1993 CD

By the summer of 1993, with Gil now a teenager, Laura was ready to return to the studio. She hadn't been prolific in recent years. In fact, she brought only six new songs to the sessions. The album's remaining tracks would be re-recordings of two earlier works (a song written for a film soundtrack, and a revised take on a number from *Mother's Spiritual*), with three more covers of her beloved early soul classics: what she refers to in the liner notes as 'the teenage primal heartbeat songs of my youth'. This would be her first album of the CD era. Since the new technology allowed tracks to be shuffled or scrambled at will, there was less incentive for the sort of careful sequencing she'd emphasised in the vinyl era. Nonetheless, she used the 'primal heartbeat songs' as a framing device to enclose her own work, which owed so much to their precedents.

For co-producer, she turned to old friend Gary Katz. Best known for his work as producer on every Steely Dan album recorded during the first run of their career from *Can't Buy a Thrill* (1972) to *Gaucho* (1980), Katz was a safe pair of hands. He'd known Laura since the late-1960s after they met through a mutual friend. They shared a love of soul music and, what's more, he had his own studio, River Sound on 95th Street in Manhattan, equipped with the latest 32-track digital setup. In an interview at the time, Laura described the appeal to Dan Backman:

He's got this really nice studio, and he can make a good, clean, professional record. He can go with an approach that's simple, and he's open-minded to a certain degree, and not a producer that is going to impose on me or try to impose on me a definite style because that would not work.

Katz assembled an impressive set of backing musicians, several of them people Laura had worked with before, like trumpet player Randy Brecker and his saxophonist brother Michael. She cut most of the tracks initially as piano/vocal with drums, bass and guitar, and then re-recorded her lead vocal over the rhythm tracks, adding her own vocal harmonies. Compared to the extended genesis of her earlier records, it seems to have been a smoother process. Laura's perfectionism may have been the only obstacle, especially at the protracted mixing stage involving three-way decisions between Laura, Katz and his regular engineer Wayne Yurgelun. Katz was perhaps being diplomatic about tension in the control room when he told John Stix years later that 'There were no downsides to working with Laura, other than her very meticulous scrutiny of her own work and what she accepted'.

Thanks to Katz's input, the production certainly had more bite than some of her recent albums: a fact she was happy to acknowledge in interviews. She explained to Rob Steen of *The Independent*: 'I definitely went for a certain kind of energy, and this little R&B band we used was a good marriage to my voice and material. Compared, say, with *Smile*, where I was seeking peace of mind, it does, um, sizzle a bit'. It doesn't sizzle like her explosive New York trilogy, but it does bring her private and public concerns together into one final statement and find a satisfying musical shape for them. Significantly, five tracks from the album were included (with her approval) on the 1997 career retrospective *Stoned Soul Picnic*, compared to just one cut ('Mr Blue') from *Nested*.

'Utterly irresistible, if slight and – as the title suggests – a little daft': even *Rolling Stone* was easing up on Laura in its review of her first studio offering for nine years. In fact, *Walk the Dog* picked up some strong notices and revived interest in Laura's work at a time when she was at risk of slipping out of view. Several TV shows pursued her – among them *Saturday Night Live* and *The Late Show with David Letterman* – hoping for a guest slot. It wasn't to be: she was never comfortable with appearing on television, much to our loss. In 1993, her piano-based rhapsodising was worlds away from the technopop of synths, samples and rhythm boxes and the impending guitar-driven grunge of Nirvana; not so much *retro* as timeless.

'Oh Yeah Maybe Baby (The Heebie Jeebies)' (Phil Spector, Hank Hunter)

Laura continued to bookend her concerts with cover versions of her favourite oldies: a practice she carried over when sequencing the new studio album. The Crystals were another of the early-1960s girl groups that lit up Laura's youth. A product of the Phil Spector production line, this rather obscure song first appeared as the B-side to The Crystals' 1961 single 'There's No Other (Like My Baby)'. Clearly, it stuck in Laura's memory. 'It kind of has a spirit to me of a new beginning – just something being born', she told Fred Migliore in a 1993 radio interview. For all its period charm, the original sounds positively robotic compared to Laura's treatment. Her version is slower, looser, more seductive. As always, when covering a song, she re-harmonises it to absorb it into her characteristic style. Multitracking her backing vocals, she creates a whole girl group out of her own voice. The effect is nuanced and rather brilliant. As her co-producer Gary Katz put it in a later interview with John Stix, 'Every moment you are working in the studio with her music, her fingerprints are all over it, her palm prints or footprints'.

'A Woman Of The World' (Laura Nyro)

A song about healing, as Laura told interviewer Fred Migliore: 'A healing in the relationship'. Perhaps there were fractures in the long-term relationship with Maria Desiderio, although the lyric seems to hint at a broader process of maturation. 'I was a foolish girl', she sings, 'Now I'm a woman of the world'. The getting of wisdom has been a 'hard lesson', but now she's learned that friends and lovers create the weather systems around one another: they make the rainfall in bad times and the sunshine in good. Human relationships as microclimate – it's a pleasing fancy, just on the right side of sentimentality.

This track – the album's longest – earns a heavy arrangement, replete with horns and strings. It's one of the stronger of her later melodies, made more interesting as ever by the way she uses *melisma* – the ornamental prolonging of one syllable over a number of notes, a key feature of gospel music that entered the pop mainstream in the 1960s with Aretha Franklin and others.

'The Descent Of Luna Rosé' (Laura Nyro)

'Dedicated to my period': that's what it says on the lyric sheet just under the song title. How many songs have been written on the subject of menstruation? Female poets will sometimes broach the topic, but Laura is surely the first – and perhaps the only – popular songwriter to take it on. As Germaine Greer wrote in *The Whole Woman*, menstruation appears to many a female like a 'troublesome tenant after whom she has to clean up'. Italian girls make him a man and call him 'Il marchese' (The marquis); German girls used to call him 'Der rote König' (The red king); in English, it's usually 'The curse'. Thankfully, the song avoids anatomical detail. Indeed, the lyric is sufficiently vague that – but for the dedication 'to my period' – the casual listener might miss Laura's drift altogether. (A Google search on the phrase 'Luna Rosé', produces in top places a brand of perfume and a rosé wine from the Napa Valley!) The track seems to be more of a plea for tolerance, addressed to her lover, as Laura faces up to premenstrual tension and waits for 'Luna Rosé' to descend. 'These blues are serious', she sings, in need of diversion. 'Tell me a joke/Make sure it's funny'. She doesn't want earnest analysis of her state – 'Baby, don't look at me like Freud' – she wants to 'lighten up', or she wants her lover to lighten up.

In fact, the whole thing may be a bit of a tease. When she spoke to *The Independent* newspaper on her last visit to the UK in 1993, interviewer Rob Steen asked her about this curious song. Her response: 'A lot of people didn't realise I was joking, sadly'. The music certainly seems determined to look on the bright side. It's breezy, upbeat, efficient, and unadventurous. According to her friend Richard Denaro, she planned at one stage to name the whole album *The Descent of Luna Rosé*. Let's be grateful she chose instead to spotlight 'Walk The Dog & Light The Light', one of the album's stronger tracks.

'Art Of Love' (Laura Nyro)
In her 350-page biography of Laura, Michele Kort devoted all of half a sentence to this track, describing it merely as a 'wish for peace'. She had the song's measure. Like motherhood and apple pie, peace is a good thing – we can all agree on that – but the lyric does little more than state the proposition. 'Let peace shine for every boy and girl', she sings. 'You and I belong to one world'. True enough. In a spoken-word interlude over instrumental backing, voices in a variety of accents bring us messages of 'peace on earth' from Tibet, Iraq, Israel, Africa, Jamaica, America, Cuba and Italy. It's all very noble, and Freddie Washington's bass-playing at least injects some urgency into proceedings, but this one was never destined to become an anthem of the peace movement.

'Lite A Flame (The Animal Rights Song)' (Laura Nyro)
After two comparatively bland tracks, the album hits its stride at last. In her later career, Laura was increasingly focused on placing her art in the service of the causes she believed in. Invariably, the song was carried forward by her sincerity. Sometimes, but not always, she went beyond and found the right-shaped musical container for that sincerity. 'Lite A Flame' is one such. Like 'The Wild World', it expresses her horror at the exploitation of animals. The chorus spells out how she places the animal rights movement on a par with the parallel struggles against racism and sexism: 'It's like prejudice/For the colour of your skin/Prejudice for a woman/Prejudice for an animal'. Speaking to Paul Zollo of *Songtalk* magazine, she explained how she'd found a musical form for her message:

> In order to say what I wanted to say, I had to tell a certain story. Somehow, the rhythm I fell into with the song was almost a rhythm that an elephant might walk in … And when I got to the chorus, I knew I was writing the song I wanted to write. A certain pattern got created with three short lines, and basically, the lines create empathy. All of these things are connected. I see racism and sexism as a lack of empathy.

The leisurely tempo does indeed convey something of an elephant's plodding gait. The song takes us from the captive animal, confined in zoo or circus, to the freedom of the elephant roaming the plains, and joins these images to human ones – the Masai matriarch on her way to the watering-place, children climbing trees, hunters slaughtering 'for greed not need'. Such itemising of detail makes for a stronger lyric than in her other issue-driven songs, which too often collapse into abstraction. Wisely, she opts for a simple arrangement of just keyboards, bass and percussion, with some overlay of real animal sounds, presumably taken from a wildlife documentary or soundtrack library.

'Louise's Church' (Laura Nyro)

A celebration of female creativity, 'Louise's Church' invokes four artists by name – Sappho, Billie Holiday, Frida Kahlo and Louise Nevelson. For Laura, the arts were interconnected, all alike sources of inspiration. In the song, she calls on these manifestations of the 'heavenly muse' or avatars of the 'goddess of life and music' to 'shine on me a while'. At the risk of pedantry, let's take them one by one.

As a poetry lover (and as someone in a same-sex relationship), Laura surely knew the work of the ancient Greek poetess Sappho of Lesbos. Perhaps she'd come across Sappho's two most famous poems: one, an address to Aphrodite in which the poetess summons the goddess and asks to be delivered from unrequited love for a girl; the other, a declaration of love for a girl, the mere sight of whom moves Sappho intensely while a young man sitting beside her seems godlike in his indifference.

In 1994, Paul Zollo asked Laura what Billie Holiday meant to her. 'I think that she is the great mother-musician, teacher of the art of phrasing', was her response. However, with Holiday, Laura responded not just to the 'real musician', as she puts in the lyric, but also to the denunciation of racism expressed in the song 'Strange Fruit', that overt protest against lynching which Holiday recorded in 1939 and continued to sing for the rest of her life. In the Zollo interview, Laura goes on to say that her own mother Gilda, though primarily an opera fan, had introduced her to Holiday's music at an early age:

> I remember her telling me about 'Strange Fruit' and telling me of the lyrics. And it's funny, because I read a couple of things in an album jacket that said when she started getting into 'Strange Fruit', that's when the music ended. And I just thought, 'I feel the opposite'; that was her art and her consciousness just travelling deeper.

This is interesting, given the development in Laura's own art from the self-absorption of her early songs to the socially conscious outlook of the later work.

A talented watercolourist herself, Laura was intensely responsive to the visual arts. In a 1984 interview, she told Bruce Pollock of a visit she'd made to New

York's Museum of Modern Art, where she found herself coming back again and again to Van Gogh's 'Starry Night' painting. 'I think my favourite songs come from a certain place of elemental power', she explained. 'Van Gogh became one with that night sky and that painting. That's what I mean by elemental power'. With the line 'Frida drew the moon', the song reminds us of another elemental power: the once-neglected art of the Mexican painter Frida Kahlo (1907-1954). Following her rediscovery in the 1970s, Kahlo became an icon of non-conformity for minority groups and political movements, and her troubling imagery seeped into the public consciousness. In many of Kahlo's canvases, sun and moon appear alongside one another. For her, the moon was a symbol of womanhood, as it was for Laura. Conversely, in the Aztec mythology that Kahlo's art drew on heavily, the sun required human sacrifice. Trust the moon, therefore. Perhaps that's why the song ends at a slower tempo, with Laura drawing out the single word 'moo-oo-oon'.

The fourth name in Laura's roll-call may be less familiar. An immigrant from what is now Ukraine, Louise Nevelson (1899-1988) became a leading sculptor of the Abstract Expressionist movement in the US. She's best known for her monumental wooden assemblages of discarded objects found on city streets. Laura had a slight personal connection to Nevelson, in that her great-uncle and great-aunt on her mother's side had been among Nevelson's first art teachers in 1920s New York, and she was evidently familiar with one of the sculptor's most famous commissions. In 1975, Nevelson designed the chapel of St. Peter's Lutheran Church, which was to form part of the new Citigroup Center in midtown Manhattan. It's an immersive environment – nine wall-mounted sculptures, white-on-white, accented with gold leaf, and enhanced by the play of shadow and light from a single window. As the lyric puts it, this is 'art of grace and style'.

'Louise's Church' sports an infectious melody, albeit supported heavily by a repetitive three-chord motif. With tight playing from the horn section and decorative flute additions, this is an album highlight. Introducing the song at a gig in Lockport, NY, in June 1990, Laura said it was about 'a group of kick-ass women artists'. It takes one to know one.

'Broken Rainbow' (Laura Nyro)
Broken Rainbow was a feature-length documentary about a subject close to Laura's heart, the mistreatment of Native American peoples. Shortly after completing *Mother's Spiritual,* she was approached by the filmmakers Maria Florio and Victoria Mudd about writing a title song for the film. As she told interviewer Fred Migliore in 1993, they sent her a five-minute clip, and immediately she knew she 'wanted to be part of it'. (The filmmakers tell the story slightly differently. In their version, she was asked to write a song on a Monday, and by Friday – 'although never having seen a frame of footage from the film' – she was singing and playing the finished composition to the director over the phone. They never changed a note or a word.) The

movie dealt with the forcible relocation of over 10,000 Navajo Indians from their ancestral lands in Northern Arizona. The US government claimed that by moving the Navajo off the land, it was settling a long-standing territorial dispute between the Navajo and Hopi tribes. The tribes denied that there was a dispute, and argued that the real forces at work were energy companies hungry to exploit mineral rights to coal and uranium. Those Navajos who'd already moved had suffered high rates of depression, stress-related disease and death. Notions of exclusive land ownership were alien to many native peoples. For them, one could no more *own* the land than own the air above the land or the rain that fell on it or the animals that lived on it. *Broken Rainbow* rightly scooped the 1986 Oscar for Best Documentary Feature, and 35 years after it was made, it still packs a punch.

The song is Laura at her best: a simple, direct utterance, perfectly aligned with the film's style. The music proceeds slowly, like an incantation, voice rising airily over broken earthbound chords. To the Navajo, the loss of earth was, in some measure, the loss of heaven. The lyric captures the reactions of the dispossessed – the old woman recalling the joy of better days, the young warriors unable to understand city living, the elders insistent that their religion 'is in these lands and skies' – and contrasts the 'home sweet home' of the American dream with the reality of the 'broken rainbow'. Maria Florio told *Cinéaste* magazine in 1986: 'What I tried to do was, basically, what I think Laura Nyro did with the music. We kept the images clean and clear, and we tried to segue from image to image through the eyes of the Indians. It wasn't so much manipulation of film on our part, as it was a follow-through on who they are'.

After initially recording 'Broken Rainbow' for the film soundtrack, Laura took the song into her live set and continued to perform it at every opportunity. It features on *Live at the Bottom Line*. In April 1990, she sang it solo on VH1's weekend *Earth Day* programming. (At the time of writing, a grainy video of that performance is up on YouTube.) The final version is the one on *Walk the Dog,* and it proved to be the quickest session for any of the album's tracks. According to engineer Wayne Yurgelun, they laid it down in a single take, late at night, with just percussion and bass to augment vocal and piano. For once, Laura resisted the temptation to re-record her vocal. When near the end of her life she worked on the career retrospective *Stoned Soul Picnic*, this was one of two 'political' songs she insisted on including; 'Lite A Flame' was the other. Sound judgement on her part – in both these tracks, social concern and musical integrity make a happy marriage.

'Walk The Dog & Light The Light (Song Of The Road)'
(Laura Nyro)

For a working musician, it's always a challenge to reconcile touring with family life. In the early-1990s when her son was still little, Laura was determined to strike that balance. She tried to limit concert engagements to weekends so she could be at home for Gil during the school week. That must've been the starting point for this track, which she subtitled 'Song Of The Road'. Laura presents herself as an independent woman, making her living, 'workin' with the gypsies' of the road, but she stops along the way to phone her boy. She's singing on Saturday night, she tells him, but she's 'headed for the city line' and she'll be home on Sunday. So he should 'Walk the dog and light the light'. The CD booklet helpfully provides a photo of the pooch in question: a friendly Belgian Tervuren sheepdog called Ember, waiting to be walked.

'Walk The Dog...' has a different sound texture from the typical Nyro track. Instead of the piano and synth that dominate the album's other cuts, this one is driven by guitars, acoustic and electric. Appropriately for a 'song of the road', the effect is to take her to a different place somehow, almost more Laurel Canyon than East Coast. It's also one of the more harmonically enterprising of her later songs. Major/minor alternations or equivocations were always a hallmark of her style; here, the flip from the Fminor9 chord to the major9 as she moves from the title line to 'I'll see you Sunday' is like a window opening. Rightly promoted to the album's title track, this is a strong evocation of the pull of home that any working mother can identify with.

'To A Child' (Laura Nyro)

A re-recording of a song from *Mother's Spiritual*, this originated as a contribution to the 1992 Columbia project *'Til Their Eyes Shine: The Lullaby Album*. Laura was in good company, her track appearing alongside offerings from Rosanne Cash (who also co-produced), Emmylou Harris, Gloria Estefan, Dionne Warwick and Carole King, among others. Like the earlier *Acoustic Christmas*, *'Til Their Eyes Shine* was a charity album; the royalties, in this case, would go to benefit children living in areas of conflict. This new version of the song begins and ends with Lou Marini's breathy flute soloing but is otherwise for piano and voice alone. Laura's songs often sounded better stripped of adornments, and such is the case here. 'To A Child' emerges from its cocoon as one of the greatest and tenderest of her later compositions.

'I'm So Proud' (Curtis Mayfield)/'Dedicated To The One I Love' (Lowman Pauling, Ralph Bass)

The album ends as it began, with cover versions. 'I'm So Proud' was a minor 1964 hit for Chicago soul pioneers The Impressions, peaking at number 14 on the singles chart. Speaking to Sweden's *City Magazine* in 1993, Laura recalled how as a teenager she used to listen 'for hours and days and weeks and months and years' to Curtis Mayfield's songs on her little record player: 'I used to find a lot of comfort in his music'. That said, her treatment of the song here is perfunctory. It hardly has time to establish its identity before she goes straight into another number, an oldie from The Shirelles. Although it barely dented the charts on first release in 1959, their version of 'Dedicated To the One I Love', re-released in 1961, reached number three on the *Billboard* Hot 100 chart. The song got a new lease of life in 1967 when The Mamas & the

Papas took it to number 2 in the singles chart. Laura gives this one much more attention than 'I'm So Proud'. As if looking back to her last Shirelles cover (with Labelle on *Gonna Take a Miracle*), she simulates a girl-group sound through multitracked backing vocals; there's a smoochy saxophone solo for Michael Brecker, and Laura holds on to the last note as if she doesn't want to let go of it. As a conclusion to the last disc to appear in Laura's lifetime, it leaves you wanting more. She has circled back to where the album started – and where *she* started – with the 'primal heartbeat' memories of her youth.

And there *was* more to come.

Angel in the Dark (2001)

Personnel:
Laura Nyro: lead vocal, harmonies, acoustic and electric piano
John Tropea: electric guitar, horn arrangements
Freddie Washington, Will Lee: bass
Bernard Purdie, Chris Parker: drums
Bashiri Johnson, Carol Steele: percussion
Randy Brecker: trumpet
Michael Brecker: tenor saxophone
Jeff Pevar: guitar
Tommy Mitchell: horn arrangements
Recorded at Gallway Bay Music, Rockland, Maine, March 1994; River Sound, New York City, October 1994; Power Station, New York City, August 1994 and April and August 1995; The Magic Shop, New York City, circa 2000
Producer: Laura Nyro
Executive producer: Eileen Silver-Lillywhite
Other production credits: Scott Billington, Wayne Yurgelun, Robert Smith, Steve Rosenthal, Albert Leusink, Dan Gellert, Peter Gallway, Daryl Gustamaccio, T. Gonz
Label: Rounder
Release date: April 2001
Chart place: Did not chart
Running time: 56:21
Current edition: Rounder 2001 CD

Given that *Walk the Dog & Light the Light* was the last album Laura released in her lifetime, in one sense, the discography ends here. By 1994, she was out of contract with Columbia and owing back taxes to the IRS after receiving bad financial advice. However, she was still a powerful draw as live performer and still fizzing with ideas for new material. She opened discussions with various people about starting a new label. Enter Eileen Silver-Lillywhite, an academic and longtime fan who'd befriended Laura after stepping onto the tour bus in 1988 and presenting a book of her own poems, *All That Autumn*, to the poetry-loving star. The pair bonded and decided to form their own independent record company, Luna Mist Records, Inc. The plan was to launch with three separate projects, which Silver-Lillywhite would co-finance – a live album derived from Laura's gigs at the Bottom Line in 1993 and 1994, another collection of oldies (a sort of *Gonna Take a Miracle 2*), and a disc of her new songs. After that, the label would release poetry recordings and music by other musicians.

Recording of the new material mostly took place in Studio A at the Power Station in Manhattan. Silver-Lillywhite describes it as being like 'a cathedral, covered in wood, large for tracking'. Typically, Laura would sing three takes of a song, then come into the control booth to listen. If she was satisfied, she'd choose one to keep. But, given her perfectionism, we'll never know whether what was ultimately released is what she would have wanted. Working with Peter Gallway and Wayne Yurgelun as co-producers, she laid down a range of solo demos and band arrangements of cover versions and new compositions. Safe pairs of hands from the *Walking the Dog*-era were encouraged to help out: Freddie Washington on bass, and Bernard Purdie on drums.

What may not have been apparent to her fellow musicians is just how ill she was by this point. (Not that you'd guess it from the assured, confident vocals preserved on *Angel in the Dark*.) After a deterioration in her health, she was finally diagnosed in summer 1995 with ovarian cancer, the same disease that had taken her mother's life 20 years earlier. Despite chemotherapy and trying every alternative treatment she could find, Laura passed away at home in Danbury on 8 April 1997. She was just 49.

There followed a legal dispute between Laura's partner Maria Desiderio and Silver-Lillywhite for possession of the master tapes from these final sessions. Silver-Lillywhite came out on top. With production assistance from Scott Billington and some *post hoc* musical additions from John Tropea and the Brecker brothers, an album was carved out of the material. Is it something Laura would have endorsed? According to Silver-Lillywhite, she wanted the music released 'no matter what happens'. Her friend Patty DiLauria disputes this, as do percussionist Nydia 'Liberty' Mata and road manager Roscoe Harring. Whatever the truth, anything of Laura's is worth hearing, even works in progress, and *Angel in the Dark* preserves some of her tenderest and most intimate studio performances.

Ironically, the reviews were better than many she received in her lifetime. Rob Hughes in *Uncut,* waxed poetic over her voice – 'snowflake-pure and time-smoothed as a beach pebble' – and her talent: 'a full-bodied vintage'. For Richard Williams in *The Guardian*, the album was 'just about everything her fans could wish for'. Comparing the 'fresh and taut' band arrangements to Van Morrison's *Moondance*, he's more generous than I would be. Still, *Angel in the Dark* is a valuable postscript to the *official* discography, and many listeners whose enthusiasm had cooled since her 1960s/1970s peak found a route back into her music through these final recordings.

'Angel In The Dark' (Laura Nyro)

Recorded at the Power Station on what would prove to be her last ever day in the studio – 5 August 1995 – this is a touching way to open the album. Reunited with members of the *Walk the Dog* band, finger-clicking to set the tempo, she settles into a slow vibe. Aside from the vocal, as mellifluous as ever, there's a delicious instrumental break for the Brecker brothers on trumpet and sax.

It sounds like a conventional love song, but according to Eileen Silver-Lillywhite, this wasn't Laura's intention. Rather, it's a prayer addressed to those she'd counted on as she grew up and the relatives who'd since died – especially her beloved mother and maternal grandfather, whose photographs she'd place on the piano to guide her. She's summoning the spirits of her ancestors, 'because the night's so long'. In a repeated chorus, she asks her guardian angel (or angels) to 'come back' to her. Although this was one of the earliest written of her new songs, its lyrics must've acquired added poignancy by the time she came to record. In 1995, she'd begun treatment, and the effects of her chemotherapy were apparent, even to the band. Different accounts describe her wearing a wig or beret to conceal hair loss. Still, her optimism shines through. Placing faith in a force outside herself personified in angel form, she looks forward to a time when 'I'll be dreamin' and on my feet again'.

'Triple Goddess Twilight' (Laura Nyro)

Laura debuted 'Angel In The Dark' at the Bottom Line on Christmas Eve 1994: 'a new song that I'm working on', she told the audience. At that point, the lyrics were slightly different from the final version, and she broke off midway to invoke the 'triple goddess'. The connection is explicit to this next track, recorded at the Power Station during a session on 28 April 1995. The guardian spirits are with her again. She remembers her mother cradling her in her arms as they picnic in the park; having written about taking her own child to the park, Laura relishes the continuity. She recalls the inspiration of grandfather Mirsky, 'working-class, urbane, street-wise', who taught her that 'We can change the world, girl'. There was an urgency about commemorating these influences, as she put it in a press kit interview for Cypress: 'I think that if a close guardian of yours like that dies, you feel like you've lost your port, and you grieve until you decide to build a strong bridge between yourself and the world and give of yourself'.

Overhanging all, in the chorus, is a presiding deity. We've already met the 'triple goddess' in 'Sophia', represented by the phases of the moon. She's often pictured as three distinct figures united in one being – the Maiden, the Mother and the Crone – each of which symbolise a separate stage in the female life cycle. These are ancient ideas, but they gained new traction in the 1960s thanks to Jungian psychology and the cult-ish popularity of Robert Graves' book *The White Goddess*, which Laura may well have come across. Graves saw the Triple Goddess, the 'White Goddess' of his title, as the muse of all lyric poetry. For Laura, each phase of her life as a woman had been creatively productive. She'd been a Maiden ('Only now am I a virgin', she sang in 'The Confession'). She'd been a Mother (carolling 'Mother's Spiritual'). Now, perhaps, she foresaw a future as 'Crone'. Despite the word's negative connotation, in new age and feminist spiritual circles a 'croning' is a ritual rite of passage into an era of wisdom, freedom and personal power.

That said, the interest here surely lies in the lyric, not in the music. This is a solo performance at the piano, with overdubbed vocal harmonies. It has the leisurely fluency of much of her later composing, as if she's just improvising over a well-worn chord sequence. Its power comes from above: the transcendent voice and the notion of a goddess in twilight.

'Will You Still Love Me Tomorrow' (Gerry Goffin, Carole King)

From the August 1994 sessions at the Power Station comes this Goffin/King classic. Originally a hit for Laura's beloved Shirelles, it had the distinction in 1960 of being the first song by a black all-girl group to reach number 1 in the United States. It got a new and well-deserved lease of life when co-composer Carole King included it on her multiplatinum-selling album *Tapestry* in 1971. The Shirelles had to accommodate the song within the three-minute confines of the pop single. Carole King's version is slower and, taking advantage of the LP format, expands to over four minutes. Hers also breathes the spirit of mature reflection rather than the hurried teenage angst of the original.

Laura had been singing this song all her life – it was on her setlist on a Japanese tour in 1972 and almost certainly featured in those youthful songfests in the New York subway. At just shy of six minutes, her studio version here is even slower than Carole King's, and very much the gentle ruminations of a woman in her 40s who knew of what she spoke. Bass, drums and percussion create a comforting bed over which Laura sketches a luxuriant vocal. Like much of the material on *Angel in the Dark*, it sounds unfinished, as if waiting for extra layers to be added – especially in the last couple of minutes – but it's still a thing of beauty.

'He Was Too Good To Me' (Richard Rodgers, Lorenz Hart)

'He Was Too Good to Me' first saw the light of day in the tryouts of Rodgers and Hart's 1930 Broadway musical *Simple Simon* but was dropped before the show's New York opening. (Goodness knows how it fitted into the plot, which revolved around a newspaper vendor who spends his time in a fairy-tale land where bad news doesn't exist.) Despite its inauspicious beginning, the song has since become a jazz standard. Laura had grown up with the Broadway songbook. She was also a devoted admirer of Nina Simone. These two influences come together in this number, which – she told a London audience in 1994 – she first learned at age 15 from a Simone live album (presumably *At the Village Gate* (1961)). 'Nina Simone sang about progressive politics, about love, intimacy, anger; she was a great artist', Laura commented in her final interview.

This studio version was laid down solo with acoustic piano at River Sound in October 1994. Apparently, there were many takes preceding the one preserved here. Each time, she'd say, 'I know I can get it better'. She follows Simone's lyric – which sometimes deviated from the Lorenz Hart original – and, as usual, adapts the harmony into her own style. The most obvious change from any previous version is that she de-genders the song. There are no he-men in her life these days. Although the original title is printed in the CD packaging and booklet (presumably for copyright reasons), her version is actually *'You Were Too Good to Me'*. All the pronouns are altered to allow for a fractured same-sex relationship. Did she have regrets? 'Everything's all messed up and wrong now', she sings. 'It's only natural that I'm so blue'. Perhaps there were tensions with Maria Desiderio that she channelled into these words. Perhaps it's prurient to enquire, now that both of them are gone. Her vocal here is from the heart, whatever prompted it.

'Sweet Dream Fade' (Laura Nyro)

The last track Laura ever recorded in the studio. By lunchtime on 5 August 1995, she and the band had completed the three songs they planned to record during the session. These were the only numbers for which written music parts had been prepared. Silver-Lillywhite suggested to Laura that 'Sweet Dream Fade' was also ready to record. Laura pulled out her journal where she'd drafted the lyrics and played the song for John Tropea, who quickly wrote up a chart. Luckily, Laura and the band were able, in Silver-Lillywhite's words, to 'slide right into the song'.

'Slide' sounds about right. There is a fluency and spontaneity here that recalls the best of her live recordings. Horn and sax decorate a laid-back vocal. Like 'He Was Too Good To Me', this is a song born of regret, hinting at a ruptured connection to a loved one; perhaps a period before Laura's illness when she and Desiderio had separated for a while. 'Never mind perfection', she sings, 'Do you wanna make a sweet dream fade?'. They both have too much to lose. She found friendship in love; now by rekindling love, she hopes to restore friendship as well. It's sad that she would never return to the studio to finish this track to her satisfaction, as it has more commercial potential than many of her later songs. Conventionally structured, with a likeable chorus and even a middle eight, it lingers in the mind.

'Serious Playground' (Laura Nyro)

It's no accident that in English, as in other European languages, we talk about *playing* music. Music and play are a hair's breadth apart. Both require creativity and imagination. To improvise – to make something where before there was nothing – we must revisit the child's openness to experience. But as adults, we do it in earnest, with consequences. In this song Laura writes about her craft, characterising songwriting in this double aspect, as a 'serious playground'. That's the ground where she works and plays. At the behest of her 'boss', the Muse, she makes her living forging 'sound architecture'. She compares singing to flying (an analogy she also used in interviews): 'So send me the music/Like wings to fly'. The lyrics eloquently spell all this out. As a musical statement, its power lies in the statement and not in the music, which is unremarkable by her standards.

'Serious Playground' was one of the demos recorded solo at the Power Station in April 1995. She got as far as adding basic harmony overdubs, but otherwise, the song is in its raw state.

'Be Aware' (Burt Bacharach, Hal David)

One of the lesser-known songs from the Bacharach/David hit factory, 'Be Aware' had its first outing on a Bacharach TV special with Barbra Streisand in March

1971. However, like so many of their songs, it was written originally for Dionne Warwick, and it's Warwick's 1972 recording that Laura is likely to have known. Its socially conscious lyric would've spoken to her very directly: 'When the sun is warm where you are/And it's comfortable and safe where you are/Well it's not exactly that way/All over'. We should be summoned out of our complacency by the need to fight loneliness in old age, to safeguard freedom of speech, to save people from homelessness – so the song tells us. (In her cover versions, Laura rarely sings an entire lyric. In this case, for whatever reason, she omits several lines about hunger in a world of plenty.)

Bacharach's original score for Streisand and Warwick was typically lush. Laura's version, recorded in the final sessions at the Power Station in August 1995, is pared down to the bone, with the rhythm section entering only on the second chorus. Of course, we don't know how much more work she would've put into these tracks had she lived. But as it stands, this is a standout piano/vocal, its honesty attuned to the simple message of universal brotherhood conveyed in the lyric.

'Let It Be Me' (Gilbert Bécaud, Manny Kurtz)

From the earlier sessions at River Sound in October 1994 comes this little gem. 'Let It Be Me' was in origin a French song, first recorded by its composer in 1955 as 'Je t'appartiens' ('I Belong To You'). The words were by one of France's most distinguished lyricists, Pierre Delanoë, who also wrote hits for Dalida, Edith Piaf, Charles Aznavour, Johnny Hallyday and many others. Equipped with a new, syrupy English lyric by Manny Kurtz, the song found its way to The Everly Brothers, who took it to number 7 on the *Billboard* Hot 100 in 1960. It's worth seeking out the French original: Delanoë's lyric with its references to 'fragile insects' and 'docile slaves' has a quaint poetry all its own. However, it's the Everlys' version with their smoochy close harmonies that launched a thousand newlyweds first onto the dance floor, and theirs is the version Laura would've grown up with.

Laura's recording is clearly a demo. What's also clear is that she's calling up the song from distant memory. In a sense, she's come full circle. At her awkward first audition with Artie Mogull, he asked her if she knew any 'standards'. She fumbled her way into several songs, unable to remember any in detail. Here – nearly 30 years later – she remembers half the words of an old favourite, rearranges the order of verses, and ends by improvising some lines of her own: 'Well, look here baby/Won't you give me a chance/'Cause look here baby, tonight's the night'. Take that, Artie!

Laura had previously recorded this number in 1990 for Columbia's *Acoustic Christmas* album. That take was a more prepared version but even more abridged, as it forms part of a short medley with 'The Christmas Song'.

'Gardenia Talk' (Laura Nyro)

A song about rebirth, filled with a touching optimism. On the page, the lyric reads as a beautiful, rather cryptic poem. The idea seems to be that, in spring, thoughts turn to love; one is inclined to 'swoon like a teenager'. Her mature self takes a broader view, however, making this more than just another love song. A vision only half-grasped before, something or someone she met 'on the bus to springtime', is now fully realised. Settled into her rural retreat, she, at last, understands the language of flowers, epitomised by 'gardenia talk'. Nature presents herself as a 'sweet stranger': gardenia plants are prized for the strong sweet scent of their flowers. A connection to Nature, and to her own sweet, strange nature, will bring the singer out of darkness. Silver-Lillywhite suggests that the sea was everything for Laura – she couldn't live without being near water; hence the lyric's reference to a dream that 'fills the darkness like the sea'.

But this is all wild surmise. Each will hear in the song what they want to hear, attending to the music within the words as well as to the words themselves. Perhaps it's enough to be 'struck by the poetry', as she puts it in the second verse. This was one of the new songs she debuted in concert in the early-1990s. (It was slated to appear on *Walk the Dog & Light the Light*, but she felt it was still unfinished). The 1994 live recording from the Bottom Line (included on *The Loom's Desire*) is in some ways more satisfactory than the one here – the three backing singers of (what Laura called her) Harmony Group flesh out her piano/vocal without obscuring the view. The studio recording made at the Power Station in August 1995, with a prominent percussion role for Bashiri Johnson, feels stuffy in comparison, lacking in the capacity for self-surprise. But, like everything on this album, it may not have come to us in the form Laura would've wished.

'Ooh Baby, Baby' (William Robinson, Jr., Warren Moore)

Smokey Robinson and the Miracles released the original version of this soul classic in 1965. Produced by Robinson and written by Robinson and fellow Miracle Warren 'Pete' Moore, 'Ooh Baby Baby' was a number-4 hit on the *Billboard* R&B singles chart and reached number 16 on the *Billboard* Hot 100. It's a familiar tale, in life as in countless soap operas – man cheats on his woman; man regrets his actions; man begs his woman to take him back. In Laura's version, recorded in August 1994 at the Power Station, she delivers the lyric more or less complete – this one doesn't require any change of pronouns – over a basic rhythm track, lightly decorated by Jeff Pevar's guitar. Like the preceding track, it lacks some of the spontaneity of live performance. (Check out the abbreviated version of the song she gave audiences in Japan in February 1994, which is preserved on *Trees of the Ages*.) But there's no denying Laura is never given her due as one of the great jazz vocalists, and the way she holds the last note in the studio recording – as if she doesn't want to let the song go – is truly inspired.

'Embraceable You' (George Gershwin, Ira Gershwin)

'She's the best I've ever been involved with. She's George Gershwin, phenomenal in a classical sense, as well as a pop sense'. That was the verdict of *New York Tendaberry* producer Roy Halee, and he wasn't alone in associating Laura's name with that of a great predecessor. Both were native New Yorkers; both were innovators, especially in expanding the harmonic idiom of popular song. But this track was Laura's only overt salute to Gershwin. 'Embraceable You' is a classic first aired in the 1930 Broadway musical *Girl Crazy*, where a young Ginger Rogers and co-star Allen Kearns performed it in a song-and-dance routine. Severed from its original context, the song quickly became a jazz standard. Laura might well have known it from her mother's LPs of Broadway show tunes or from Billie Holiday's 1944 recording.

It's another solo demo from the August 1994 sessions at the Power Station. Laura performs only the first chorus and slows the tempo right down. Not surprisingly, 'Come to papa' in the published lyrics becomes 'Come to mama'. As usual, she substitutes her own wide-voiced chords for Gershwin's originals – a habit that unmoors the song curiously. Without the pleasing inevitability of Gershwin's cadences and harmonic progression, this invitation to romance feels less cosy, as if hinting at trouble ahead.

'La La Means I Love You' (Thomas Randolph Bell, William Hart)

Hailing from Philadelphia, male vocal trio The Delfonics had one of their most enduring successes with this number. The song hit number 4 in the *Billboard* pop charts in 1968 and was a number-19 UK pop single in 1971. Many cover versions followed, including one by Laura's friend Todd Rundgren (on his 1973 album *A Wizard, a True Star*).

The studio recording comes from the band sessions on 29 August 1994, with Laura switching to electric piano. It's more worked out than some other tracks on this album; there's even an embryonic instrumental break at 2:18, and she leans into the chorus as if those la-la-la's really mean something. She delivers the original lyric in its entirety while making adjustments that transform hetero into same-sex attraction. 'Many guys have come to you' becomes 'Many *loves* have come to you'. The line 'If I ever saw a *girl* that I needed in this world' didn't require changing (although, in a slip of memory, it comes out as 'If there ever was a girl').

This song had been in her repertoire for a while. *Live at the Bottom Line* (drawn from the summer-1988 shows) concludes with a medley combining 'La La Means I Love You' with 'Trees Of The Ages' and 'Up On The Roof'. In early-1994, she recorded another version, this time as a guest vocalist with The Manhattan Transfer for their 1994 album of collaborations, *Tonin'*. It was a further chance to work with Arif Mardin, her co-producer on *Christmas and the Beads of Sweat*. With heavy strings and squeaky-clean vocal harmonies, the Manhattan Transfer's version has a blander arrangement than Laura would've gone for herself, but her unmistakable vocal in the first verse lifts the whole track out of mediocrity.

'Walk On By' (Burt Bacharach, Hal David)

Another Bacharach/David song written originally for their muse Dionne Warwick. Like the best of Hal David's lyrics, it tells a story in a few well-chosen words. The singer has broken up with her lover. Pride – 'foolish pride' as the song has it, all she has left – prevents her from showing how much she's hurting, so she wants to be left to 'grieve in private'; her ex should just 'walk on by'. Warwick's version was released in April 1964 and reached number 6 on the *Billboard* Hot 100 and 9 in the UK. 'Walk On By' would become Warwick's second international million-seller, following 'Anyone Who Had A Heart' earlier in 1964 – a year in which Warwick had a remarkable *six* US chart hits in all. Her version is so familiar, with its little trumpet motif in the verse and those major-7ths on piano in the chorus, that it's a brave soul who takes it on.

This was one of the first demos Laura recorded with Peter Gallway at Gallway's studio in March 1994. She reduces the accompaniment to a simple piano vamp. As so often in these cover versions, the interest lies in her vocal – the upward tilt she gives to the melody in the chorus, the inflection on the words 'broken and blue' to suggest they come from experience. Under her fingers, the harmonic reworking may have become predictable, but the voice continued to surprise.

'Walk On By' was a regular in her concerts. There are live versions from December 1970 on *The Nights Before Christmas*, from May 1971 on *Spread Your Wings and Fly*, and from February 1994 on *Trees of the Ages: Laura Nyro Live in Japan*. Every time, she sings it differently. The early versions, true to the spirit of the early studio albums, are marked by stark contrasts: they're dramatic; some might say histrionic (I say exciting). In Japan, two decades later, it's a calmer, more reflective performance, as if she's grown into the song.

'Animal Grace' (Laura Nyro)

This slight track is probably a tribute to Laura's dog Ember, whom she'd already celebrated in 'Walk The Dog & Light The Light'. With it, she returns to one of her favourite themes: animal welfare. We're all part of a great chain of being – dogs, birds, humans – and it'll take a 'change of mind', she says, to recognise that fundamental truth. The second verse invokes the name of St. Francis of Assisi, friend to the animals. One story she may have had in mind describes how, while Francis was travelling with some companions, they came to a place in the road where birds filled the trees on either side. Francis told his companions to wait for him while he went to preach to 'my sisters the birds'. The birds surrounded him, captivated by the power of his voice, and not one of them flew away. The saint is often portrayed with a bird, typically in his hand.

Possibly an unfinished composition, 'Animal Grace' was laid down solo during the April 1995 Power Station sessions. Laura developed it only as far as adding vocal harmonies on the final lines: 'The earth is/An interspecies affair'. Some have noted the similarity here to the chorus of 'Family Affair', a US number-1 for Sly and the Family Stone in 1971. If intentional, it's a neat joke, rounding off a light-touch treatment of a serious subject.

'Don't Hurt Child' (Laura Nyro)

Optimism is always so inspiring when we encounter it in the seriously ill. Seemingly addressed to her son Gil who was by now a teenager, this is a song of consolation and encouragement. The boy's suffered some reverse, some moral injury. Never mind, she says, 'Heal your wild wing/And fly'. A summer storm will clear the air. She knows this because she's been there: 'I was young and wild once too', she reminds him. Sentiments any parent can identify with are here expressed without artifice, and the effect is rather touching. We know the 15-year-old Gil fell foul of the law (drug offences) and received a two-year probationary sentence. There would be more turmoil in his young life before he found his feet as an adult. Active nowadays as a rapper (under the name Gil-T), he finds that performing brings him closer to his mother and her musical legacy.

The basic track of 'Don't Hurt Child', one of the last songs Laura wrote, was recorded in early August 1995 at the Power Station. It's another medium-slow ballad, a gentle rumination poised over the simplest of chordal accompaniment. To bring colour, John Tropea deploys a loaned 1938 Martin and adds jazz flourishes with his own hollow-body L5 Gibson (the same guitar he used when playing with Laura in the 1970s), although some or all of his parts may have been overdubbed later when the album was being prepared for release: the CD liner notes don't make this clear.

'Coda' (Laura Nyro *et al.*)

The listener might be forgiven for thinking that's the lot. The 'Coda' appears to be just over a minute's reprise of the chorus from the title track: 'Come back to me, come back'. But the CD runs on (unless, assuming it's finished, you switch it off), and after three minutes of silence, a hidden track surfaces at the 4:05 mark. Unannounced and uncredited in the CD booklet, this is actually a couple of verses of 'Come And Get These Memories', an old Martha and the Vandellas number that Laura had been singing in concert since at least 1972. It's a shame she doesn't get deeper into it, as it's going swimmingly when it peters out after 90 seconds. When Cherry Lane Music published a volume of Laura's collected lyrics in 2004, they were caught out by this one: Eddie Holland's lyrics for Holland-Dozier-Holland are dutifully printed in the book as if they were an original Nyro composition. Somehow, there's poetic justice there. All her life, she'd reinterpreted the 'teenage primal heartbeat' songs of her youth and drawn on them as a source for her own music; now she waves goodbye to us with an oldie that could be mistaken for a newbie.

The (Posthumous) Live Albums

No one who ever saw Laura perform live will forget the experience. Her concerts were as near to revivalist meetings as anything else. Her fans treated her – and continue to treat her after death – with almost religious devotion. For someone who could appear introspective and self-absorbed on stage, these live appearances were a vital connection to her audience. As she told British journalist Penny Valentine in 1971, 'I feel very clean when I've finished, even though I'm really a funky mess when I come off stage. I think whenever you feel love, you feel cleansed'. She said little to the audience between songs. When she spoke, the contrast between her quiet, almost whispering tone and the powerful singing voice could be startling.

Live recordings capture some of the best of Laura, especially later on. It's notable that the early live shows are all solo, quite distinct from her studio work. The arrangements on her New York trilogy would've been difficult to reproduce live. As her style became less idiosyncratic, it was better adapted to working with a live band: unpredictable tempo-change and *rubato* can be a nightmare for sidemen looking to the singer for their lead. In later years, she liked to use an electric keyboard rather than a stage piano, which enabled her to face the audience rather than sit at right angles to them. (Not that pianist-showmen like Elton John or Jerry Lee Lewis ever felt inhibited by their acoustic instrument!) Behind the smaller keyboard, Laura felt closer to the audience. There is a loss, though: no electronic keyboard in her day could replicate the velocity-sensitivity or expressive range of an acoustic piano.

In addition to the two live albums that appeared in her lifetime, there's been a spate of posthumous releases. The recordings vary in quality. Some were originally radio broadcasts; others were taken from the soundboard. None – with the possible exception of *The Loom's Desire* – were sanctioned by her for release, so they form a kind of appendix to the official discography. In chronological order of performance, below is the tally to date.

The Nights Before Christmas: New York Broadcast 1970
Released on Unicorn 2020 CD
An FM radio broadcast from Bill Graham's legendary Fillmore East venue on 22 December 1970. At this solo gig, Laura was supported by then-lover Jackson Browne. The Fillmore East on 6th Street and Second Avenue in the East Village had been an old Loews movie house. For a venue able to hold over 2,600 people, it was surprisingly intimate, and you get that sense from the recording. The sound quality is not optimal, and an unfortunate tape glitch (at 8:12) mars the mounting tension in 'Map To The Treasure', but these are rare chances to hear tracks from the New York trilogy, stripped down.

Spread Your Wings and Fly: Live at the Fillmore East, May 30, 1971
Released on Sony/Columbia Legacy 2004 CD

For this later solo gig, she shared the bill with Spencer Davis and Peter Jameson. It was less than a month before the venue closed its doors forever. Photographer Amalie R. Rothschild, who took pictures on the night, recalled the event: 'She had an elegant little table next to her, with a pitcher of water and a vase with a few flowers. It was just her, with the audience right there, in this magical environment'.

The recording was made with three microphones mixed directly to a stereo tape machine. Considering its lo-fi origins and the brittle state of the sole surviving tape, the mastering team did wonders with this. Laura was deep in recording *Gonna Take a Miracle* at this point – a fact obvious from the setlist, which has little overlap with *The Nights Before Christmas* and includes more cover versions. It's a fabulously unbuttoned performance from Laura.

Live at Carnegie Hall: The Classic 1976 Radio Broadcast
Released on All Access 2012 CD
Season of Lights wasn't the only memorial of Laura's four-month tour in support of the *Smile* album. We also have this concert from 31 March 1976, broadcast live on New York radio station WNEW-FM and WBCN-FM in Boston. Although not her first appearance at Carnegie Hall, this was reportedly the first live radio broadcast by a pop artist from New York's most prestigious concert venue. Audience members were handed daffodils as they arrived, so that when stepping on stage, Laura was faced with an ocean of flowers. Some of the exuberance of earlier performances is gone. In its place is an air of mature re-evaluation, of emotion recollected in tranquillity. Symbolic of this shift is how a lyric is subtly altered – in 'Upstairs By A Chinese Lamp', the 'man who takes her sweetness' has now become the '*one* who takes her sweetness'.

This release is to be approached with scepticism. The balance between soloist and backing is, like the sound quality generally, not ideal. And at several points – 'When I Was A Freeport', for example – the compilers have used the selections from Carnegie Hall that are already available on *Season of Lights*. The remainder may have been taped off-air.

American Dreamer: Live at the Bottom Line, 12th July '78
Released on Air Cuts 2016 CD
Another broadcast, this one from a syndicated radio show on KBFH-FM. 'Both of us are happy to be here tonight', the heavily pregnant Laura tells her adoring audience before launching into 'Rhythm And Blues', one of the punchier cuts in this 50-minute solo set. Other numbers – mostly drawn from the recently released *Nested* album – are more meditative, but she mixes in classics like 'Sweet Blindness' and 'Emmie', making this a useful addition to the live recordings.

A health warning: don't read the liner notes before playing the CD. The booklet lacks any credits, and by way of background, merely reprints a couple of snooty reviews of the gig from the *New York Times* and *Village Voice*. As evidence of how some critics in 1978 still didn't *get* her, these may have historical value, but they're a lousy introduction to this life-affirming music.

Newport Folk Festival 1989
Released on Lexington 2016 CD

Laura was never really a folkie, but then, the Newport Folk Festival had broadened its remit over the years to take in other genres. Laura's sole appearance there came over two decades after the notorious 'Electric Dylan' controversy, when the great troubadour plugged in and set folk purists' teeth on edge.

Also on the bill that August weekend in 1989 were B.B. King, John Lee Hooker, Odetta, John Prine and Emmylou Harris. Laura's short set was broadcast on community radio station KGNU-FM. She has the same band with her as on *Live at the Bottom Line*, and the setlist is similar, with one intriguing exception: she revisits 'Eli's Comin''. Since the only lines she uses are 'Hide your heart, girl' and 'She walked, but she never got away', the song is reduced to a husk of its 1960s self. With a final cry of 'She walked!', Laura seems to be signalling that all that man trouble is behind her now.

Live from Mountain Stage (1990)
Released on Blue Plate Music 2000 CD

Mountain Stage is a music radio show that first aired in 1983. Recorded before a live audience, it's produced by West Virginia Public Broadcasting and distributed worldwide by National Public Radio (NPR). Laura's appearance, dating from 11 November 1990, was presumably recorded at the show's home base, the Culture Center Theater in Charleston, West Virginia. It's a short solo set, barely more than 30 minutes. The unforgiving digital piano does her no favours, which is a pity, as the recording quality is higher than in many of the posthumous releases, and she's in fine voice. The audience is respectful, although this crowd don't exhibit the cultic devotion she'd known in earlier years. She previews three numbers that will appear on *Walk the Dog & Light the Light*: two covers and the new original 'Lite A Flame'. These are intimate, stripped-down performances that capture where she was in 1990: in a quiet place. Evacuated of drama, even 'And When I Die' (introduced as 'one of the first songs I ever wrote, many moons ago') sounds resigned as much as defiant.

Laura Nyro Live: The Loom's Desire (1993/94)
Released on Rounder 2002 CD

A new live album was one of the three projects Laura began to develop with her friend Eileen Silver-Lillywhite. Without the artist's supervising presence, this two-disc release is the closest approximation we have to how she wanted it to sound. Christmas was a special time of year for Laura. To perform on Christmas Eve had become a tradition with her – 'Her gift to her city, to her hometown' in Silver-Lillywhite's words – and here we have her yuletide sets from the Bottom Line, New York City, in two consecutive years. By this stage, she liked to work entirely with other female musicians: her 'Harmony Group' she called them. With these singers – six in 1993, three in 1994 – she could recreate the spirit of her teenage doo-wop vocalising on street corners. At the Bottom Line, she sang with the Harmony Group for part of each show, and solo with piano for the rest. Alas, these would be her last-ever appearances in her native city.

The 1994 concert included two new songs that she'd record in the studio the following year, 'Angel In The Dark' and 'Gardenia Talk'. Otherwise, the setlists drew on a fair cross-section of her past work, with emphasis on the more recent albums. A surprise inclusion in 1994 was 'Save The Country', a song to which she no longer felt very connected. She explained to Paul Zollo of *SongTalk* magazine how it came about:

A friend of mine asked me, like, 20 times to sing it. And then, finally, I sang it in a completely different way, and I was just at one with the song. I sing it with my voice lower and edgier. I used the essence of the song. I found renewal with the song, totally to my surprise.

If anything, her voice had grown stronger and more assured with time, especially in the middle and lower registers. It's a mature voice, well-matched to soulful newer songs like 'Angel In The Dark'; perhaps less so to 'Save The Country', where the 'fury in my soul' now sounds like a distant memory.

Incidentally, the album title *The Loom's Desire* is a beautiful phrase from 'Emmie', surely one of her lyrics that could stand alone as a poem. It suggests a union of craft and Eros. The songwriter, like the weaver, fashions an object of desire out of the warp and weft of their fabric. It aptly describes Laura's art.

Trees Of The Ages: Laura Nyro Live in Japan (1994)
Current edition: Omnivore 2021 CD
Laura's 1994 tour took her back to Japan for the first time in over 20 years. Clad in a silk kimono and tabi (the traditional Japanese socks worn with thonged footwear), she visibly embraced a culture she loved. Her Japanese fans were conspicuously younger than the audiences she now had in the US or Britain, and according to Diane Garisto – a backing singer on the Japan trip – Laura jokily referred to these gigs as her 'Puppy Love tour'.

A selection of live recordings appeared in the West in 2003 as *Laura Nyro: Live in Japan*. A more comprehensive collection of 21 tracks was originally issued only in Japan but is now finally available worldwide. Drawn from three concerts in Osaka and Tokyo in February 1994 (the majority from Osaka), these are highly professional recordings using multiple microphones. They capture the full resonance of the grand piano as it rises to meet the rich timbre of her voice. On 'Wind', a song she'd recorded with Labelle in 1971, the three backing singers join her in a joyous *a cappella*; elsewhere, they fill in upper harmonies or trade lines back and forth with Laura. Never exactly garrulous between songs, she tries out a few words of Japanese on her audience. How much of her English they understand is an open question. 'Is there an animal rights movement in Japan?', she asks rhetorically as she launches into 'Lite A Flame'. In 1994, when the Japanese government was still seeking to oppose a ban on commercial whaling in the Southern Ocean, she was hoping for a yes.

Trees of the Ages is one of the best of the posthumous releases, a fitting memorial to Laura at her late peak.

Afterthoughts

Why has Laura Nyro dropped out of view? Once upon a time, her name was up there among the groundbreaking singer-songwriters of the era, or of any era. Take it from those who know, like Elton John, in conversation with Elvis Costello on the *Spectacle* TV show (Channel 4 UK, CTV Canada) in 2008:

> I idolised her ... She influenced more songwriters – and successful songwriters – than any other songwriter ... This is music so far ahead of its time that still sounds… unbelievable – the soul, the passion, just the out-and-out audacity of the way her rhythmic and melody changes come, was like nothing I'd ever heard before.

Or Joni Mitchell, in an interview on BBC Radio 1 in May 1983:

> You know, they try to put you into groups and schools, like to put you in some kind of neat filing system. Of all of the filing systems that I went into, Laura was one of the rare ones whose company I enjoyed. She's a great artist, you know, a complete original.

Or Alice Cooper, interviewed by *American Songwriter* magazine in October 2020:

> Laura Nyro is my favourite songwriter of all time. Listen to her *Eli* album. That is *amazing* songwriting. I have worn out all of her albums. And even with all of the people who have covered her songs, nobody does them better than her. And I don't know how she does it, but she comes up with some of the most unique lyric lines that I have ever heard in my life. It's almost *Porgy and Bess*. It's got this strange quality. Nobody writes like her.

One day when Laura was just starting out, singer Odetta came to meet her and to hear 'And When I Die'. The older woman's reaction was spontaneous and enthusiastic: 'Genius' was Odetta's word for it. Bob Dylan was a fan, too. Columbia boss Clive Davis tells a story of throwing a party for Janis Joplin after the wayward chanteuse played Madison Square Garden in December 1969. When Dylan – another guest – found out that Laura was also at the party, he asked to meet her. Laura was too tongue-tied to speak. For once, Dylan had to keep the conversation going by himself, telling her how much he was 'into her albums' and 'admired her music'.

One reason for Laura's relative eclipse is that she wouldn't play the fame game. Disillusioned with the music industry, she dropped out for a while. Her muse tempted her back in the late-1970s, but by then, the business had changed and she had changed. Something of the old intensity was gone – what the critic Ian MacDonald called her 'strong, reality-modifying sense of a personal interpretation of life' – to be replaced by a more detached sense of self and a new commitment to causes. Although those causes are worthy in themselves, great art is rarely born out of propaganda: preaching is best left to preachers. When the *New York Times*' William Kloman interviewed Laura back in 1968, she offered to cook him lunch. The canned elephant meat heated for *hors d'oeuvres* had turned out badly, so she gave it to her dog Beautybelle instead. Kloman commented: 'Laura is fond of elephants, so had been eager to see what they tasted like'. That's an extraordinary statement to read 50 years later, in our eco-conscious times. In a sense, her journey from *eating* elephants to *saving* elephants is the story of her career as songwriter – from ingesting experience to mapping the world as it is. My own preference for the music made by the carnivorous Nyro over the vegetarian one will have been obvious. Still, I'd never question another person's life choices, and I don't question hers.

What never changed was the loyalty of her fans. To this day, they cherish her memory with worshipful fervour, play her albums and swap anecdotes of concerts attended. Now as then, her music registers particularly with women and with gay and lesbian audiences. Her biographer Michele Kort has described how Laura's songs – redolent of female mystery and desire – triggered her own same-sex longings and encouraged her to confront subterranean urges. But Laura's appeal isn't limited to any one group of people, nor would she have wanted it to be. As her friend Richard Denaro commented, 'She felt that to say someone was gay or lesbian or bisexual was merely another form of separatism, and there was enough separatism without that'.

The beautiful face that gazes downward on the front cover of *Eli* – patterned after a Renaissance Madonna – is the face of a contemplative. 'Mary kept all these things, and pondered them in her heart', as Luke's Gospel has it, following the angel's visitation to the Virgin. Laura's corpus of work is a deep pondering, unusual in popular music. That's just one of many ways in which she expanded the territory. The critic Charlotte Greig has praised her bravery in incorporating the experience of motherhood into her work. Greig stresses how difficult this can be for women musicians, comparing Laura favourably to Patti Smith, whose response to the tensions and conflicts of being a mother was to pen 'unbelievably twee songs' about 'little blue shoes'. Greig concludes: 'It sometimes seems that in rock, the more radical and rebellious the artist's adolescent pose, the more conventional and trite their adult writing eventually becomes'. Laura ran that risk without succumbing.

Perhaps something is stirring. Billy Childs' superb 2014 album *Map to the Treasure* is one of the most lavish and resourceful tributes that one artist has ever paid to another. And in 2021, when Madfish issued a deluxe box set of Laura's first seven studio albums on vinyl, it prompted more retrospective coverage than she'd received in years, as journalists competed to locate her spiritual legacy in everyone from Tori Amos to Kate Bush. Let's hope her time has come again. In any case, thanks to her recordings, she lives on inside me and inside all those whose lives she has touched with her music.

Bibliography

Bertei, A., *Why Labelle Matters* (University of Texas Press, 2021)

Calello, C., Austin T., *Another Season: A Jersey Boy's Journey with The Four Seasons and Beyond – The Memoirs of Charlie Calello* (Really Big Coloring Books, 2018)

Davis, C., Willwerth, J., *Clive: Inside the Record Business* (William Morrow, 1975)

Greig, C., 'Female Identity and the Woman Songwriter' in *Sexing the Groove: Popular Music and Gender*, ed. Sheila Whiteley (Routledge, 1997)

Hoskyns, B., 'Dark Angel: Laura Nyro' in *God is in the Radio: Unbridled Enthusiasms, 1980-2020* (Omnibus, 2021)

King, T., *The Operator: David Geffen Builds, Buys, and Sells the New Hollywood* (Random House, 2000)

Kort, M., *Soul Picnic: The Music and Passion of Laura Nyro* (St. Martin's Press, 2002)*

LaBelle, P., Randolph, L., *Don't Block the Blessings: Revelations of a Lifetime* (Riverhead, 1996)

MacDonald, I., 'The Artistry of Laura Nyro' in *The People's Music* (Pimlico, 2003)

Neal, M., 'Bellbottoms, Bluebelles and the Funky-Ass White Girl' in *Songs in the Key of Black Life: A Rhythm and Blues Nation* (Routledge, 2003)

Nyro, L., *The Music of Laura Nyro* (Warner Bros Publications, 1971)

Nyro, L., *Time and Love: The Art and Soul of Laura Nyro* (Cherry Lane Music, 2002)

Nyro, L., and others, *Laura Nyro: Lyrics and Reminiscences* (Cherry Lane Music, 2004)

Romanowski, P., 'Laura Nyro' in *Trouble Girls: The Rolling Stone Book of Women in Rock*, ed. B. O'Dair (Random House, 1997)

Rudden, P., 'Stacking the Wax: The Structure of Laura Nyro's Studio Albums' in *Singing for Themselves: Essays on Women in Popular Music*, ed. P. Rudden (Cambridge Scholars Publishing, 2007)

Stix, J., ed., *The Laura Nyro that I Knew: Stories from Bandmates and Friends* (Self-published, 2020)

Taylor, D., *Prisoner of Woodstock* (Thunder's Mouth Press, 1994)

Weller, S., *Girls Like Us: Carole King, Joni Mitchell, Carly Simon – and the Journey of a Generation* (Washington Square Press, 2008)

*Kort's bibliography lists most of the interviews and contemporary profiles I have quoted from.

Index of Song Titles

Key to abbreviations:

AD   *Angel in the Dark*
CBS   *Christmas and the Beads of Sweat*
ETC   *Eli and the Thirteenth Confession*
GTM   *Gonna Take a Miracle*
LBL   *Live at the Bottom Line*
MND   *More than a New Discovery*
MS   *Mother's Spiritual*
N   *Nested*
NYT   *New York Tendaberry*
S   *Smile*
SL   *Season of Lights (Live)*
WDLL   *Walk the Dog & Light the Light*

The abbreviation means that the song is discussed in the chapter of that title, not that the song necessarily appears on the album as released. All songs are by Laura Nyro except where marked with an asterisk.

Ain't No Mountain High Enough* GTM
Ain't Nothing Like The Real Thing* GTM
American Dove GTM
American Dreamer N
And When I Die MND
Angel In The Dark AD
Animal Grace AD
Art Of Love WDLL
Beads Of Sweat CBS
Be Aware* AD
Been On A Train CBS
Bells, The* GTM
Billy's Blues MND
Blackpatch CBS
Blowin' Away MND
Brighter Song, The MS
Broken Rainbow WDLL
Brown Earth CBS
Buy And Sell MND
California Shoeshine Boys MND
Captain For Dark Mornings NYT
Captain Saint Lucifer NYT
Cat-Song, The S
Child In A Universe N
Children Of The Junks S

Christmas In My Soul CBS
Christmas Song, The* LBL
Coda* AD
Coffee Morning S
Companion LBL
Confession, The ETC
Crazy Love N
Creepin'* MS
Dancing In The Street* GTM
December's Boudoir ETC
Dedicated To The One I Love* WDLL
Descent Of Luna Rosé, The WDLL
Desiree* GTM
Don't Hurt Child AD
Eli's Comin' ETC
Embraceable You* AD
Emmie ETC
Enough Of You MND
Free Thinker, A MS
Gardenia Talk AD
Get Me My Cap S
Gibsom Street NYT
Go Find the Moon MND
Goodbye Joe MND
Hands Off The Man (Flim Flam Man) MND
He's A Runner MND
He Was Too Good To Me* AD
High Heeled Sneakers* LBL
I Am The Blues S
I'm So Proud* WDLL
I Met Him On A Sunday* GTM
I Never Meant To Hurt You MND
In And Out MND
In The Country Way NYT
It's Gonna Take A Miracle* GTM
Japanese Restaurant Song, The LBL
Jimmy Mack* GTM
La La Means I Love You* AD
Late For Love MS
Lazy Susan MND
Let It Be Me* AD
Light – Pop's Principle N
Lite A Flame (The Animal Rights Song) WDLL
Lonely Women ETC

Louise's Church WDLL
Lu ETC
Luckie (First version) MND
Luckie (Final version) ETC
Mama Roux* N
Man In The Moon MS
Man Who Sends Me Home, The NYT
Map To The Treasure CBS
Mars SL
Melody In The Sky MS
Mercy On Broadway NYT
Midnite Blue S
Money S
Monkey Time* GTM
Morning News, The SL
Mother Earth GTM
Mother's Spiritual MS
Mr. Blue (The Song Of Communications) N
My Innocence N
Nest, The N
New York Tendaberry NYT
Nowhere To Run* GTM
Oh Yeah Maybe Baby (The Heebie Jeebies)* WDLL
Once It Was Alright Now (Farmer Joe) ETC
Ooh Baby Baby* AD
O-o-h Child* GTM
Park Song LBL
Polonaise* MS
Poverty Train ETC
Refrain MS
Rhythm And Blues N
Right To Vote, The MS
Roadnotes MS
Roll Of The Ocean LBL
Save The Country NYT
Serious Playground AD
Sexy Mama* S
Smlle S
Someone Loves You S
Sophia MS
Spanish Harlem* GTM
Springblown N
Stoned Soul Picnic ETC
Stoney End MND

Stormy Love S
Sweet Blindness ETC
Sweet Dream Fade AD
Sweet Lovin' Baby NYT
Sweet Sky, The N
Talk To A Green Tree MS
Time And Love NYT
Timer ETC
To A Child MS, WDLL
Tom Cat Goodbye NYT
Tom Dooley* CBS
Trees Of The Ages MS
Triple Goddess Twilight AD
Up On The Roof* CBS
Upstairs By A Chinese Lamp CBS
Walk On By* AD
Walk The Dog & Light The Light (Song Of The Road) WDLL
Wedding Bell Blues MND
When I Was A Freeport And You Were The Main Drag CBS
Wild World, The LBL
Wilderness, A MS
Will You Still Love Me Tomorrow* AD
Wind, The* GTM
Woman Of The World, A WDLL
Woman's Blues ETC
Women Of The One World LBL
You Don't Love Me When I Cry NYT
(You Make Me Feel Like) A Natural Woman* GTM
You've Really Got A Hold On Me* GTM

Joni Mitchell - *on track*
every album, every song

Peter Kearns
Paperback
160 pages
35 colour photographs
978-1-78951-081-1
£14.99
$21.95

Every album and every song by this legendary Canadian singer-songwriter.

In her long career, Canadian songstress Joni Mitchell has been hailed as everything from a 1960s folk icon to 20th century cultural figure, artistic iconoclast to musical heroine, extreme romantic confessor to both outspoken commentator and lyrical painter. Eschewing commercial considerations, she simply viewed her trajectory as that of any artist serious about the integrity of their work. But whatever musical position she took, she was always one step ahead of the game, making eclectic and innovative music.

Albums like *The Ladies Of The Canyon*, *Blue*, *Hejira* and *Mingus* helped define each era of the 1970s, as she moved from

exquisitely pitched singer-songwriter material towards jazz. By the 1980s, her influence was really beginning to show via a host of imitators, many of them big names in their own right. He profound influence continues in popular music to this day.

This book revisits her studio albums in detail from 1968's *Song to a Seagull* to 2007's *Shine*, providing anecdote and insight into the recording sessions. It also includes an in-depth analysis both of her lyrics and the way her music developed stylistically over such a lengthy career, making this the most comprehensive book on this remarkable artist yet written.

Elton John 1969 to 1979 - *on track*

every album, every song

Peter Kearns
Paperback
144 pages
35 color photographs
978-1-78952-034-7
£14.99
USD 21.95

Every track recorded by music legend Elton John during the 1970s, arguably his most creative and most commercial successful period.

In 1970, Elton John, formerly Reginald Kenneth Dwight, stepped from the obscurity of suburban Pinner, Middlesex, England, into a pop culture reeling from post-Beatles fallout, to become one of the biggest-selling recording artists in the world. To date he has sold over 300 million records from a discography of 30 studio albums, four live albums, over 100 singles, and a multitude of compilations, soundtracks and collaborations. He is the recipient of six Grammys and ten Ivor Novello awards, was inducted into the Rock and Roll Hall of Fame in 1994, appointed a Commander of the Order of the British Empire in 1995 and knighted in 1998. In 2018 he embarked on what is intended to be his swansong world tour, *Farewell Yellow Brick Road*.

This book covers the period from Elton's earliest 1960s releases to his final 1970s album, *Victim of Love*. It is a critical overview of every track on the thirteen studio albums released in an era when Elton was at his most successful and that many fans consider to be the musical high-point of his career. Also included are the two live albums *17-11-70* and *Here and There*, and the trove of album-worthy B-sides that augmented the discography along the way.

Aimee Mann - *on track*
every album, every song

Jez Rowden
Paperback
160 pages
39 colour photographs
978-1-78951-036-1
£14.99
$21.95

**Every album and
every song by the
innovative Californian
singer-songwriter.**

Any consideration of the songwriting craft would be incomplete without the inclusion of American singer/songwriter Aimee Mann. From her first steps as singer and bass player with 1980s synth pop band 'Til Tuesday, who scored a massive MTV hit with 'Voices Carry' in 1985, she has continually produced starkly autobiographical songs, with a sense of melody that cuts through the emotional detail.

With a career now spanning almost forty years, she has built a catalogue of nine studio albums, from debut *Whatever* to 2017's *Mental Illness*, since going solo in the early 1990s. Via a series of record label frustrations, Aimee has developed into a fiercely independent recording artist,

flying outside the mainstream. Her critical acclaim has never wavered, however, and while happy to continue working in a niche market, her soundtrack for the film *Magnolia* and the accompanying Oscar nomination raised her profile considerably, adding to her stalwart army of fans.

This book gives an overview of Aimee Mann's career from her earliest days when she 'made it big' with 'Til Tuesday, through her solo career, investigating every recorded track. It is a comprehensive guide for fans and new listeners keen to investigate a double Grammy winner who is also a true original and whose work deserves to be much more widely recognised.

On Track series

Alan Parsons Project – Steve Swift 978-1-78952-154-2

Tori Amos – Lisa Torem 978-1-78952-142-9

Asia – Peter Braidis 978-1-78952-099-6

Badfinger – Robert Day-Webb 978-1-878952-176-4

Barclay James Harvest – Keith and Monica Domone 978-1-78952-067-5

The Beatles – Andrew Wild 978-1-78952-009-5

The Beatles Solo 1969-1980 – Andrew Wild 978-1-78952-030-9

Blue Oyster Cult – Jacob Holm-Lupo 978-1-78952-007-1

Blur – Matt Bishop – 978-178952-164-1

Marc Bolan and T.Rex – Peter Gallagher 978-1-78952-124-5

Kate Bush – Bill Thomas 978-1-78952-097-2

Camel – Hamish Kuzminski 978-1-78952-040-8

Caravan – Andy Boot 978-1-78952-127-6

Cardiacs – Eric Benac 978-1-78952-131-3

Eric Clapton Solo – Andrew Wild 978-1-78952-141-2

The Clash – Nick Assirati 978-1-78952-077-4

Crosby, Stills and Nash – Andrew Wild 978-1-78952-039-2

The Damned – Morgan Brown 978-1-78952-136-8

Deep Purple and Rainbow 1968-79 – Steve Pilkington 978-1-78952-002-6

Dire Straits – Andrew Wild 978-1-78952-044-6

The Doors – Tony Thompson 978-1-78952-137-5

Dream Theater – Jordan Blum 978-1-78952-050-7

Electric Light Orchestra – Barry Delve 978-1-78952-152-8

Elvis Costello and The Attractions – Georg Purvis 978-1-78952-129-0

Emerson Lake and Palmer – Mike Goode 978-1-78952-000-2

Fairport Convention – Kevan Furbank 978-1-78952-051-4

Peter Gabriel – Graeme Scarfe 978-1-78952-138-2

Genesis – Stuart MacFarlane 978-1-78952-005-7

Gentle Giant – Gary Steel 978-1-78952-058-3

Gong – Kevan Furbank 978-1-78952-082-8

Hall and Oates – Ian Abrahams 978-1-78952-167-2

Hawkwind – Duncan Harris 978-1-78952-052-1

Peter Hammill – Richard Rees Jones 978-1-78952-163-4

Roy Harper – Opher Goodwin 978-1-78952-130-6

Jimi Hendrix – Emma Stott 978-1-78952-175-7

The Hollies – Andrew Darlington 978-1-78952-159-7

Iron Maiden – Steve Pilkington 978-1-78952-061-3

Jefferson Airplane – Richard Butterworth 978-1-78952-143-6

Jethro Tull – Jordan Blum 978-1-78952-016-3

Elton John in the 1970s – Peter Kearns 978-1-78952-034-7

The Incredible String Band – Tim Moon 978-1-78952-107-8

Iron Maiden – Steve Pilkington 978-1-78952-061-3

Judas Priest – John Tucker 978-1-78952-018-7

Kansas – Kevin Cummings 978-1-78952-057-6

The Kinks – Martin Hutchinson 978-1-78952-172-6

Korn – Matt Karpe 978-1-78952-153-5

Led Zeppelin – Steve Pilkington 978-1-78952-151-1

Level 42 – Matt Philips 978-1-78952-102-3

Little Feat – 978-1-78952-168-9

Aimee Mann – Jez Rowden 978-1-78952-036-1

Joni Mitchell – Peter Kearns 978-1-78952-081-1

The Moody Blues – Geoffrey Feakes 978-1-78952-042-2

Motorhead – Duncan Harris 978-1-78952-173-3

Mike Oldfield – Ryan Yard 978-1-78952-060-6

Opeth – Jordan Blum 978-1-78-952-166-5

Tom Petty – Richard James 978-1-78952-128-3

Porcupine Tree – Nick Holmes 978-1-78952-144-3

Queen – Andrew Wild 978-1-78952-003-3

Radiohead – William Allen 978-1-78952-149-8

Renaissance – David Detmer 978-1-78952-062-0

The Rolling Stones 1963-80 – Steve Pilkington 978-1-78952-017-0

The Smiths and Morrissey – Tommy Gunnarsson 978-1-78952-140-5

Status Quo the Frantic Four Years – Richard James 978-1-78952-160-3

Steely Dan – Jez Rowden 978-1-78952-043-9

Steve Hackett – Geoffrey Feakes 978-1-78952-098-9

Thin Lizzy – Graeme Stroud 978-1-78952-064-4

Toto – Jacob Holm-Lupo 978-1-78952-019-4

U2 – Eoghan Lyng 978-1-78952-078-1

UFO – Richard James 978-1-78952-073-6

The Who – Geoffrey Feakes 978-1-78952-076-7

Roy Wood and the Move – James R Turner 978-1-78952-008-8

Van Der Graaf Generator – Dan Coffey 978-1-78952-031-6

Yes – Stephen Lambe 978-1-78952-001-9

Frank Zappa 1966 to 1979 – Eric Benac 978-1-78952-033-0

Warren Zevon – Peter Gallagher 978-1-78952-170-2

10CC – Peter Kearns 978-1-78952-054-5

Decades Series

The Bee Gees in the 1960s – Andrew Mon Hughes et al 978-1-78952-148-1

The Bee Gees in the 1970s – Andrew Mon Hughes et al 978-1-78952-179-5

Black Sabbath in the 1970s – Chris Sutton 978-1-78952-171-9

Britpop – Peter Richard Adams and Matt Pooler 978-1-78952-169-6

Alice Cooper in the 1970s – Chris Sutton 978-1-78952-104-7

Curved Air in the 1970s – Laura Shenton 978-1-78952-069-9

Bob Dylan in the 1980s – Don Klees 978-1-78952-157-3

Fleetwood Mac in the 1970s – Andrew Wild 978-1-78952-105-4

Focus in the 1970s – Stephen Lambe 978-1-78952-079-8

Free and Bad Company in the 1970s – John Van der Kiste 978-1-78952-178-8

Genesis in the 1970s – Bill Thomas 978178952-146-7

George Harrison in the 1970s – Eoghan Lyng 978-1-78952-174-0

Marillion in the 1980s – Nathaniel Webb 978-1-78952-065-1

Mott the Hoople and Ian Hunter in the 1970s – John Van der Kiste 978-1-78-952-162-7

Pink Floyd In The 1970s – Georg Purvis 978-1-78952-072-9

Tangerine Dream in the 1970s – Stephen Palmer 978-1-78952-161-0

The Sweet in the 1970s – Darren Johnson 978-1-78952-139-9

Uriah Heep in the 1970s – Steve Pilkington 978-1-78952-103-0

Yes in the 1980s – Stephen Lambe with David Watkinson 978-1-78952-125-2

On Screen series

Carry On... – Stephen Lambe 978-1-78952-004-0

David Cronenberg – Patrick Chapman 978-1-78952-071-2

Doctor Who: The David Tennant Years – Jamie Hailstone 978-1-78952-066-8

James Bond – Andrew Wild – 978-1-78952-010-1

Monty Python – Steve Pilkington 978-1-78952-047-7

Seinfeld Seasons 1 to 5 – Stephen Lambe 978-1-78952-012-5

Other Books

1967: A Year In Psychedelic Rock – Kevan Furbank 978-1-78952-155-9

1970: A Year In Rock – John Van der Kiste 978-1-78952-147-4

1973: The Golden Year of Progressive Rock 978-1-78952-165-8

Babysitting A Band On The Rocks – G.D. Praetorius 978-1-78952-106-1

Eric Clapton Sessions – Andrew Wild 978-1-78952-177-1

Derek Taylor: For Your Radioactive Children – Andrew Darlington 978-1-78952-038-5

The Golden Road: The Recording History of The Grateful Dead – John Kilbride 978-1-78952-156-6

Iggy and The Stooges On Stage 1967-1974 – Per Nilsen 978-1-78952-101-6

Jon Anderson and the Warriors – the road to Yes – David Watkinson 978-1-78952-059-0

Nu Metal: A Definitive Guide – Matt Karpe 978-1-78952-063-7

Tommy Bolin: In and Out of Deep Purple – Laura Shenton 978-1-78952-070-5

Maximum Darkness – Deke Leonard 978-1-78952-048-4

Maybe I Should've Stayed In Bed – Deke Leonard 978-1-78952-053-8

The Twang Dynasty – Deke Leonard 978-1-78952-049-1

and many more to come!

Would you like to write for Sonicbond Publishing?
We are mainly a music publisher, but we also occasionally publish in other genres including film and television. At Sonicbond Publishing we are always on the look-out for authors, particularly for our two main series, On Track and Decades.

Mixing fact with in depth analysis, the On Track series examines the entire recorded work of a particular musical artist or group. All genres are considered from easy listening and jazz to 60s soul to 90s pop, via rock and metal.

The Decades series singles out a particular decade in an artist or group's history and focuses on that decade in more detail than may be allowed in the On Track series.

While professional writing experience would, of course, be an advantage, the most important qualification is to have real enthusiasm and knowledge of your subject. First-time authors are welcomed, but the ability to write well in English is essential.

Sonicbond Publishing has distribution throughout Europe and North America, and all our books are also published in E-book form. Authors will be paid a royalty based on sales of their book. Further details about our books are available from www.sonicbondpublishing.com. To contact us, complete the contact form there or email info@sonicbondpublishing.co.uk